*Awaken the winning qualities used
by the world's most successful people.*

What's

So Special

About

YOU?

By

Coaching Specialist
Christopher Healy

77 PUBLISHING

What's So Special About You?

COPYRIGHT

This book/eBook or portions thereof may not be reproduced or used in any form or by any electronic or mechanical means, including information storage and retrieval systems, without the expressed written permission of the publisher, 77 Publishing Inc except for the use of brief quotations in a book/eBook review.

Copyright © 2020 by Christopher Healy.

ISBN: 978-0-9917273-4-6

DISCLAIMER AND/OR LEGAL NOTICES: The information in this book/eBook is distributed on an "as is" basis, without warranty. Although every precaution has been taken in the preparation of this work, neither the author nor the publisher nor affiliates shall have any liability to any person or entity with respect to any loss or damage caused or alleged to be caused directly or indirectly by the information contained in this book/eBook. The information presented herein represents the view of the author as of the date of publication. Because of the rate with which conditions change, the author reserves the right to alter and update his opinion based on the new conditions. The book/eBook is for informational purposes only. While every attempt has been made to verify the information provided in this book/eBook, neither the author nor his affiliates/partners assume any responsibility for errors, inaccuracies or omissions. Any slights of people or organizations are unintentional. If advice concerning legal or related matters is needed, the services of a fully qualified professional should be sought. This book/eBook is not intended for use as a source of legal, accounting OR medical advice. Any reference to any person or business whether living or dead is purely coincidental.

All rights reserved. The information in this book/eBook is distributed on an "as is" basis, without warranty. Although every precaution has been taken in the preparation of this work, neither the author nor the publisher shall have any liability to any person or entity with respect to any loss or damage caused or alleged to be caused directly or indirectly by the information contained in this book/eBook.

DEDICATION

To my dear wife Shirley and my boys William and Nicholas:

I dedicate this book to Shirley who has for decades been my tower of strength and love and has offered undying support in helping me with this massive work, and in the face of great odds. Thank you, sweetheart!

And for my two boys William, aged 18 and Nicholas aged 13, may they take the wisdom of these pages to heart and learn to soar high with eagles and live life with the grace of angels.

ACKNOWLEDGMENT

A very special Thank You:

To Cheryl Cowie who for months and months and months painstakingly edited my 600-page manuscript down into two readable books. She offered inspiring contributions to this work that made all the difference. Her efforts were epic, unwavering, dedicated and filled with love. Thank you from the depths of my heart.

CONTENTS

Copyright .... *i*
Dedication .... *ii*
Acknowledgment .... *ii*
Table of contents .... **Error! Bookmark not defined.***iii*
Foreword .... *vi*
To the reader .... *viii*
Preface *1*

Which leads me to the 77 Global Village. 1

What's so special about this book? 5
The Secret Sauce Within This Book 6
What can business people learn from show-business people? 12
What can anyone who wants to be happy and successful learn from this book? 16
Self Assessment Challenge How do you rate with the best? 18
77 Qualities Online Course 23

Know Thyself 27

So what is success? 28
People with a mindset of abundance are generally: 34
People with a mindset of scarcity are generally: 35
Our first week in class 40
Your assessment challenge How do you rate with the best - ROUND 1 42
The Power of Visualization 46

Facing Inner Fear 58

FAKE EVIDENCE APPEARING REAL 62

Letting Go 67

How do you rate with the best – ROUND 3 69

Procrastination 76

How do you rate with the best – ROUND 4 79
Procrastination 81
How to identify if you are a procrastinator 81

Breaking The Habit 84

How do you rate with the best – ROUND 5 86

Stuck In The Trenches 90

How do you rate with the best – ROUND 6 92
The bottom line: 94

Facing Inner Risk 96

How do you rate with the best – ROUND 7 98

All The World's A Stage 102

How do you rate with the best – ROUND 8 105

Eat. Drink. Enjoy! 108

How do you rate with the best – ROUND 9 109
Eat. Drink. Enjoy! 113
Why drink water? 114
Nutritious foods 116

Epilogue: 120

How do you rate with the best – FINAL ROUND 10........................... 123
Where do you fit on the scale? 127
In conclusion: What's So Special About YOU? 128
CLASSIC LOSERS ON THE JOURNEY TO SUCCESS!......... 131
What's so special about... NUMBER 77 134
What's so special about... Christopher Healy.. 135

What's So Special About You?

FOREWORD

I remember the nine of us standing tightly together in a 5x5 taped out square; this was our lifeboat and the imaginary object that would force out our inhibited personalities. Below us roared the deep, cold and hungry ocean, waiting patiently for its next visitor to be swallowed up. The rule was announced as each of us struggled to keep our balance within the tight space. *"Only three of you can live, the others will be pushed into the shark-invested waters!" Let the game begin!*

Suddenly our fellow students became our competitors. The war to survive had begun, and it would be the fittest or most strategic that had the greatest chance to win. The hope I held onto was luck and prayer. As the shark circled the boat waiting patiently for his next victim, the tension and screams grew as we pushed against one another trying to stay balanced on the boat. Some of the students tried to dominate their section by pushing with their bodies to force their fellow students to fall off. The fear of falling into the angry ocean filled with ravenous sharks was terrifying, and no one was giving up easily. Until it happened, the moment that life changed and I was pushed and fell into the water.

The scene continued as I walked away from the stage and sat down. Feeling discouraged and disinterested in watching my fellow students continuing their struggles in the acting exercise, I chose to sit quietly asking myself, why I was even taking this class and what this was all about. Suddenly a voice yelled out, *"What are you doing?" "You gave up!" "You get yourself back on that boat and don't you ever give up like that again!"*

For a moment I felt like crying, and my heart ached, not because I felt hurt, but because I realized I did give up. I gave up on giving it my all because I didn't believe in me. Perhaps this was because I didn't grow up with a dad who cheered me on as a young girl. Regardless, I doubted me and only saw the option to fail and not succeed. That was obvious because I based my outcome on having luck with prayer and nothing else. I was playing a small game in my life, a little fish afraid to swim with the sharks.

What's So Special About You?

Those soul touching words that woke me up came from the extraordinary man who wrote this book. Mr. Christopher Healy believed in me and did not accept anyone being mediocre in his class.

Ask yourself if you have ever felt like giving up because you didn't believe you had the ability and someone else was better.

The journey you are about to take will be as transforming as the words that once yelled out to me *"Don't you ever give up like that again!!"* You will discover what limits you and what will make you access the power that sits inside you waiting to be expressed. This book is your gift, and you will see the superstar that you really are and that there is no one quite as extraordinary or a special as you in the world.

The man that will bring your heart and soul to life is the man that has been my incredible acting coach, friend, my mental training coach and a big believer in me and thousands of others. He is a man of impeccable integrity, creativity, passion, compassion, a true visionary, a man that never gives up on people and his belief in what is possible. ***A dreamer who gets into action and changes people's lives.***

The man behind all of this is Mr. Christopher Healy, and he is about to teach you what can be possible for you. Believe me, your mind creates barriers, and Mr. Healy will show you how to take them down, be self-expressed and live in your power!

All it takes is to believe in yourself with conviction, and anything is possible. Take this from me, the woman today who holds 3 Guinness World Records running the greatest distance on a Treadmill in 12 hours. I will never give up again and neither will you after you read this book. Open your heart and soul to possibility and be ready for what you will receive.

With Gratitude,

Theresa Dugwell

3 Time Guinness World Record Holder. Peak Performance Results Coach. Co-Author, Power Source for Women, Proven Fitness Strategies, Tools and Success Stories & How to Love Your Body & Embrace Your Life.

What's So Special About You?

TO THE READER

Be assured that by reading this book, and working yourself through the step-by-step strategies and empowering qualities of the world's most successful people, you will expose yourself to a new world of happiness and wealth.

But first, let me start by telling you what has gone into making this book so you will know what you're going to get out of it. How it's going to change your life ~ guaranteed.

This book is the culmination of twenty years of my personal experiences and study on the subject of human behavior into "achieving personal success," along with ten years of direct research for this book. I have read hundreds of books, thousands of articles, attended seminars, workshops, retreats, conducted interviews and added to all that, my twenty plus years of teaching "acting courses" and Public Speaking to students from all over the world on the topics of confidence, leadership and achieving personal success in life and career.

The work that has gone into this book has consumed my life, particularly the last five years. My rewards, however, are that I believe I have assembled a vortex of information that will reveal to you how to actually overcome your weaknesses and attain your deepest wish.

This book is a catalyst to your life's rewards, offering you the success qualities, strategies and the principles used by the world's most successful people that changed their lives, and now, this knowledge is available here so you can change yours.

What's So Special About You?

PREFACE

In 2021, the world is awakening like never before. Your old ways must change to the new ways. It's time to learn how to embrace this awakening to create abundance in your life. That is what the world's most successful people would advise you to do.

Learn how to embrace this awakening to create abundance.

You know there is an ancient tale, a mystical story, of a land behind the Himalayas full of peace and harmony where an isolated people live preparing for the day when the world will be ready to live in peace. Here the wisdom of humanity is conserved, ready to save the world when needed.

Which leads me to the 77 Global Village.

In the bright light of positive perception that inspires, motivates, informs and helps you discover your wholeness, wellness and wealth, I along with some dedicated people have created a social media site named 77 Global Village. A true community that reflects our values of wholeness, wellness, and wealth. A place where you can meet like-minded people, contribute, share and experience joy. A safe place where you can explore what's so special about you? We believe, success is achievable, community is essential and humanity is good.

The 77 Global Village is the space where you will learn how to embrace this new global awakening so you can create abundance in your life like never before.

Visit www.77GlobalVillage.com

What's So Special About You?

The big idea behind this book is simple. Years ago, I asked myself "How are the world's most successful people so finely tuned into the frequency of success?" Little did I know how hard, yet "life-changing," answering that big idea was going to be.

I started acting in 1975 when I took my first acting class in school, and I have never looked back. To date, that's now just over 40 years of my life. Along the way, I worked as an actor, writer, stage manager, director, producer, artistic director, public speaker, teacher, high-performance coach, presenter, and entrepreneur. I use the most advanced power principles of Human Needs Psychology and strategic intervention in learning and personal achievement. My work is arts-based experiential learning that I call Awareness Creates Change.

My teaching background is as former Artistic Director of the Toronto Academy of Acting for Film and Television for 16 years. Also based on the "Sandford Meisner technique" of acting, human behavior, Stephen Covey – author of The Leader in Me / 7 Habits of Highly Effective People, the pioneering works of Cloe Mandanes and Anthony Robbins, founders of the Robbins-Madanes Center for Strategic Intervention, of which I am a personal member.

What I learned in all these years is that to achieve success, you must rise above others and life's challenges to develop qualities and disciplines that the average person fails to develop. To be successful, one must be prepared to change on many personal levels - *to transform*.

I believe that to reach high in life, one must reach deep into themselves to discover and amplify their own personal best efforts. You see, it's all relative - acting, business, life, and your own personal success, all comes down to who you are, what you want, the choices you make, and why you make them. Your single most important factor in achieving success is the kind of person you have to become.

My personal mission now was that I wanted my courses to reflect those "success" ingredients because learning to be an actor without the master keys to success is limited at best. I wanted my students to be able to apply their newly acquired skills into acting or into any other future career in the marketplace because not all of them will be actors.

What's So Special About You?

My courses have evolved over the decades, especially for my full-time students, from which this book was inspired. I designed my course like a flight-test simulator, which takes the students along a three-act structure called the "Hero's Journey." More on this a little later.

I also designed the course like the Marine's Paris Island boot camp course, including using the toughest part of the Marine's training, which is called the "Crucible," otherwise known to the recruits as "Hell week." My course gets more demanding as each week rolls by, and the students can feel the stakes being raised; building up their fears of hell week, except its name in my course is the "Gladiatorial Games."

In watching my students struggle to get through this course, I observed (as many times before), students facing their own inner fears, and if they really wanted what they claimed they wanted, how hard were they prepared to work? What inner fears were they prepared to face and overcome to live their dreams?

I would see on their faces a sense of "shock and awe" that seemed to wash over them as they realized that this nine-weeks was going to be one of the most challenging and decisive moments in their lives. Yes, they were going to be trained as 'actors,' but that was just one part of the "success equation" that I was offering. I was also offering them an opportunity to replace "negative behavioral habits" that held them back from their dreams, with the successful character qualities used by the world's most successful people. However, the catch was that they were going to learn through actual experience and to _apply consistently_ what they were learning in order to achieve success.

The course places the students with the daily leadership responsibilities of having a starring role in a movie or a series. The demands of that person are daunting and exciting. Each day, until he or she is finished, the "star" must carry the responsibility for the success or failure of the project. When a young actor wants to be a lead in a movie or a TV series, they have no idea of the "realities" until they step into my course. I run the course like they have a lead role for 9 weeks of shooting, which means no sick days and no sleep-in days.

Each student is on set every morning, on time and completely ready to begin the work. They have to offer up their personal best each day and "live up" to the demanding realities of what they want for themselves, which is to live their dreams.

For the students, it's a position of real responsibility with real benefits and rewards. If they survive and thrive throughout the nine weeks, they will receive an impressive letter of recommendation, a high grade on their graduation, pride of accomplishment and most importantly the knowledge of knowing they have what it takes to live their dreams.

The other alternative for the students is that they can quit the course at any time with no refund. The truth is, there is no successful middle ground in life or in business, and show business is one of the toughest industries in the world. It's definitely NOT for everybody, nor is it for self-deluded slackers.

What remained then were individuals determined to reach the top of the mountain together. They faced the reality of their dreams, their inner fears, procrastination, and laziness. They would learn to "Ditch the crap" and reach deep within themselves and learn to offer up their full potential and take responsibility for their own futures. Actually, in this book you are reading now I will show the student's journey only as a brief guide to emphasize the most empowering point, which is the "success qualities" at work and how life changing they will be *once applied*.

However, if you would like to get into the student's personal journals and get their full day by day journey of overcoming adversity then check out the book *"Life Lessons From An Acting Class."*

I, as the teacher, will offer my students the teachings, guidance, and wisdom on how to get where they want to be, how to *separate themselves from the pack, work hard towards their dreams, navigate their way through the Status Quo and play the game really smart.* At the end of the day, though, it's the students and *yourself* who make the final decisions on how this is all to play out.

WHAT'S SO SPECIAL ABOUT THIS BOOK?

Imagine this; how different your life would be if you adopted as your own, the same beliefs as the billionaire personalities of Richard Branson or Oprah Winfrey?

There is a truth, and it has been tried, and tested, and proven 100%, over and over again; that the fastest and most effective way to become successful in your life and career is to learn, and learn to apply *consistently*, the success characteristics, strategies, and principles of the world's most successful people.

The most unexpected part of all this dynamic insight and learning is that it's all revealed through the endeavors of a class of 17 – 21-year-old students, courageous enough to go through a unique 9-week intensive acting course. This course would test and push the students beyond their "perceived" limits and fears, and into discovering their true identities. What they were really made of? What was so special about each of them which they could offer to the world?

So whether you are an entrepreneur, an executive, a manager, a sales clerk, or just a "regular" person, and yes, even if you want to be an actor, you will be empowered by how powerful, relevant and poignant the sharing of their struggles, their failures, and their *achievements are to your own success*.

Ultimately, this book has the proven ingredients to change your life and offers you greater returns on your book purchase price. More importantly, though, is the "time and energy" you invest in working through these pages. It offers you the best returns of all because the truth must be...*you are worth it!*

You + Awareness + Purpose + Vision = ANYTHING!

What's So Special About You?

THE SECRET SAUCE WITHIN THIS BOOK

I'm going take you the reader on a ride for a few pages, so you get the context of the "secret sauce" within this book. So stay with me because when the "penny drops," it will drop for you.

The story of *Gilgamesh* is an epic poem from ancient Mesopotamia and regarded as one of the earliest literary writings in the world. It originated as a series of Sumerian legends (12 clay tablets) of poems in cuneiform script dating back to the early 1800 - 1150 BC. The story is about Gilgamesh, the "mythological" Hero-King of Uruk, and his half-wild friend, Enkidu, as they undertake a series of dangerous quests and adventures leading to Gilgamesh's search for the secret Elixir of immortality after the death of his friend.

This epic story has been passed down from culture to culture by word of mouth over open fires for centuries. It has influenced young kids everywhere, particularly kids like Julius Caesar, Alexander (the Great), a boy later to be known as King David, Genghis Khan, Marco Polo, Herman Cortez, Leonidas - King of Sparta, and many, many others; who have all gone forth to shape *(for good or bad)* world history.

So what is it about the Epic Story of Gilgamesh that has inspired so many lives to create so much change, and has lasted for thousands of years, and has been retold over and over again by all the great writers and filmmakers and storytellers of all time, and is today revered by those in the highest echelons of education throughout the world?

And, why is this all so important for you here, now, today?

What's So Special About You?

The "secret sauce" written within the text of this epic story is a specific set of *12 story plot points* that are laid out in a *three-act structure* known today as "The Hero's Journey."

The Hero's Journey is a structured narrative identified by the American scholar Joseph Campbell and is told in drama, storytelling, myth, religious ritual, and psychological development. The Hero's Journey describes a typical adventure of the archetype known as "The Hero," which is the person who ventures out and achieves great deeds on behalf of the community, tribe, or civilization.

The Hero's Journey carries the ingredients which resonate deeply within the human psyche. Its unique mixture has stirred up the fiery passions of humankind throughout the ages. In fact, the Hero's Journey has influenced and shaped world history more so than any other global event since the biblical story of the great flood.

Below is the Hero's Journey showing the 12 story plot points taken from the Epic Story of Gilgamesh. Please read along, and you will see how it all relates to you.

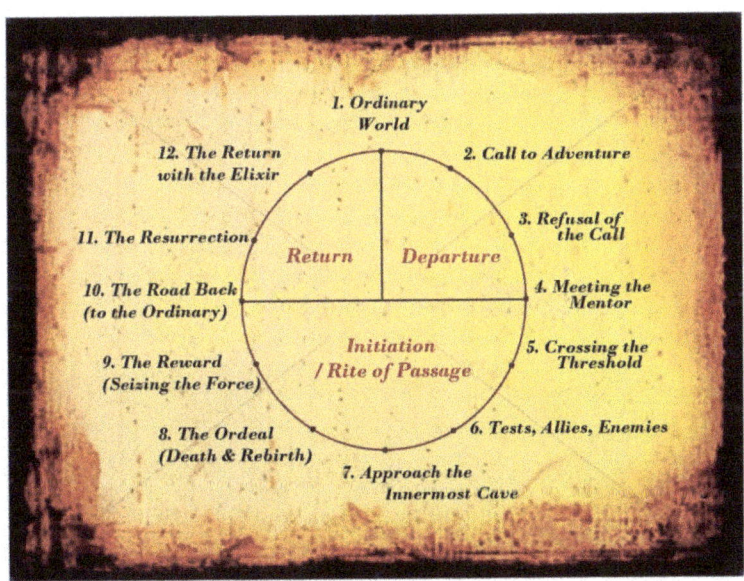

What's So Special About You?

You will find the ***recipe*** of the Hero's Journey in books written by all the masters including Kipling, Hemingway, Joyce, Twain, Tolkien, Poe, Victor Hugo, T.S. Eliot, Mary Shelley, J. K. Rowling, and this list goes on and on and on. In fact, the secret sauce is within the pages of 95% of all the books and comics you have ever read and 99% of all the movies and TV shows you have ever seen. Hollywood screenwriters are masters at telling the Hero's' Journey over and over again.

The reason is that the Hero's Journey works in firing up the human spirit like nothing else, and the secret sauce rakes in billions of dollars in entertainment each year.

The secret sauce connection is simple to understand: Humans have an instinctive love for the *ordinary man or woman who is thrust into extraordinary situations*. Here they must face challenges, confront the dark shadows within the depths of their soul and come out fighting to discover that they are *special like no other* and that this adventure is revealed to be their calling, *their destiny*. They only have to accept the challenge, do the journey and live their destiny, but most people surrender to the fears of the unknown, or to fears that the task is too impossible but the truth must be: *Impossible is Nothing!*

> The Gods called your name
> and the seas turned dark;
> the earth quaked with power.
>
> You looked up at Olympus
> screaming at the gates;
> "What will I become?"
>
> The Gods fell silent, then-
> with a thunderous roar replied;
> "Who are you now?"
>
> — Achilles

In the film "Troy," Brad Pitt plays the mythological warrior "Achilles," and in one particular scene, Achilles is preparing to fight a giant warrior of a man. A young boy hands Achilles his shield and says *"He's a Thessalonian you are fighting. He's the biggest man I've ever seen. I wouldn't want to fight him."*

What's So Special About You?

And Achilles replies *"That's why no one will remember your name."*

Can't you feel why a young lad named Julius Caesar would have jumped up with his sword and yelled: *"Follow Me!"* Or what would have inspired young Marco Polo to claim his special destiny and journey from Europe into Asia?

Whether they know it or not, people everywhere live vicariously through the Hero's Journey and "feel" what it's like to walk the path of the Titans and to feel special enough to have their own "Calling."

And primarily they "live it" knowing they will never truly experience such power for real, because they are "ordinary," and **it's this *belief* that is at the core of their chains… their *self-told lie.***

By contrast, the world's most successful people don't believe that lie. They feel a "specialness" deep inside that compels them to accept the calling like a true Titan, and no matter what the odds are stacked up against them YOU will remember their name.

Have you ever felt special deep inside?

Let's review the Hero's Journey in relation to this book which is your journey IF you choose to accept the calling.

1. You are an ordinary person living in your ordinary world.

2. You pick up this book where you are offered an opportunity, a *call to adventure*.

3. Your inner critic *refuses the call* telling you that *"You're wasting your time. You will never do this stuff. You're too busy."* However, your intuition tells you to take the challenge.

4. Reading the book, you realize that the book has become *your mentor* and guide to help you on your path.

5. You take the leap of faith by *crossing the threshold* and dare to take on the challenges within; fighting your fears, your doubts, your impatience, and begin slaying your inner demons.

6. The journey reveals *tests, allies, and enemies.* In fact, this rite of passage reveals where your inner allies (confidence and/or your relationships) support you and where your inner enemies' (your Ego and or your relationships) hinder you.

7. As you continue the journey, you are drawn into *your innermost cave,* the core of who you are, and come face to face with Good versus Evil. (You versus your negative self)

8. Your ordeal to follow results in you releasing the old self and the old ways, slaying the Dragon if you will and in that revelation you have experienced your *"Death & Rebirth."*

9. Then your *Reward* is the force of empowerment, and your new way of life is a *force that is seized* by the new you.

10. When you have finished this book, you will go back on *the road to your ordinary world,* your everyday life.

11. You return to the life of old habits, old relationships, same old – same old, negativities, and attitudes but they are no more. Your old world has changed *because YOU have changed (you are the resurrection).*

12. You have *returned with an Elixir;* a powerful *new belief* forged by the experience of the Hero's journey that you choose to walk through the pages of this book *and take on the challenges,* conquering your fears and doubts and pushing onwards to such empowering levels of consistent achievement that reflect whatever you want this power to reflect.

So my question to you is: are you up for the calling? No pressure now, but just so you know, the Hero's Journey is the story of Noah, Moses, Jesus, Julius Caesar, Mohammed *(peace be upon him)*, Napoleon, Lenin, Gandhi, David Ben-Gurion, Einstein, Edison, the Wright brothers, Bill Gates, Steve Jobs and other Titans that have *bestride the narrow world like a Colossus!*

In fact, the Hero's Journey can be claimed by anyone who ever walked life's path of tribulations and faced adversity head-on, only to walk out the other side forever a changed person.

What's So Special About You?

To walk that journey means you have walked in the steps of Titans and you can do it again. However, not everyone chooses to do it, look at Romeo and Juliet. They killed themselves. However, suicide is not for you because YOU are going to be a Titan!

Therefore, you can read this book and take the 10-rounds of assessments, discover some new weaknesses you never realized you had or find more strengths. Most people will have a "good read," and that's it, while others will take on a few of the challenges and soon enough their staying power will fade away. Some will actually take on at least one challenge and take it to the max of empowerment; changing their life for the better. Others will take on even more. It's all up to you, but the more weaknesses you challenge yourself to take up to empowering levels, the deeper you go, and the deeper you go, the more of the Hero's Journey you will emotionally encounter, and you will feel it.

I challenge you to put yourself through the eye of the empowerment needle and walk out a Titan. This book will test you. I promise. That's how I built my courses, and that's how I built this book. In a sense, my teaching was secondary to the primary experience which was about having the students walk the Hero's Journey through a series of challenges and scenarios, to help them overcome their fears and experience their power rise up in the BELIEF - *I AM SPECIAL. I AM WORTH IT.*

After all, someone once said that if you can overcome your fears, then nothing can hold you back. I believe this to be true of you and of me.

So do yourself the honor and turn your weaknesses into challenges and seek to reach the empowerment levels to the max. You have nothing to lose except mediocrity. However, you do have your destiny to claim.

What's So Special About You?

WHAT CAN BUSINESS PEOPLE LEARN FROM SHOW-BUSINESS PEOPLE?

Well according to Richard Olivier, former director of the Globe Theatre (UK) and author of Inspirational Leadership, Henry V and the Muse of Fire: "*Logical planning and implementation have got business where it is. However, it will not take it where it needs to go in this millennium. The call for flexibility, imagination, and creativity at work is growing every year. And these are the mainstays of the creative artist. As we say to the business folk we work with: 'Actors and artists have lived with insecurity for hundreds of years. Now it's your turn!'*"

To quote the Wall Street Journal 8/19/03: "*The arts are emerging as a role model for business and government organizations because the arts excel in areas where managers struggle the most: chaos, diversity, ambiguity, envisioning the future and the ability to dare to break molds.*"

> **"Anyone in business is in Show business."**
> Robin Sharma
> (Author: The Monk who sold his Ferrari)

Ultimately, did the students learn how to be actors? Yes of course, and I will add that they were fabulous performers at that. However, I would also like to add that below is the list of what else they discovered about themselves in their journey, in which they had to face and identify weaknesses and then make improvements:

- Poor communication skills
- Lack of a professional work ethic
- Lack of being consistent
- Lack of maintaining momentum
- Fear of being authentic
- Fear of failure
- Fear of taking risks
- Fear of being uncomfortable
- Fear of public speaking
- Fear of responsibility
- Fear of making mistakes
- Inability to motivate themselves
- Unable to exploit an opportunity

What's So Special About You?

- Low self-esteem
- Overreacting to issues
- Inability to lead and make decisive decisions particularly under pressure
- Inability to listen to instructions carefully
- Early on they showed a lack of working effectively with others
- Failure to consider the consequences of actions
- Inability to think carefully before making decisions
- Failure to think critically or practically on many occasions
- Failure to think flexibly about problems
- Refusal to admit mistakes or errors
- Judging self or others negatively
- Complaining about life in general or about people or circumstances or even about how unlucky you are
- Consistently procrastination
- Self-Limiting beliefs, emotions, and attitudes
- Self-Limiting thoughts focused on what's not working or on wishful daydreams
- Excuses that prevent one from moving forward

Now to a business executive reading the list above, he or she will immediately recognize that these issues run rampant through their own organizations, from top-level management down through the ranks. However, the advantages of going the distance through my program yielded the students the winning characteristics of the world's most successful people in terms of: how they think, know themselves on a deeper level, correct their weaknesses, overcome their inner fears, amplify their strengths, trust their intuition, seek opportunity, and take the correct actions needed to get successful results quickly and consistently. For example: as well as overcoming the earlier list of their flaws, they also added the benefits below that they learned, and learned to apply with professional efficiency:

- They were prepared to make drastic personal changes to how they think and behave
- Developed a professional mindset and excellent work ethic
- Were able to work with rejection

What's So Special About You?

- Nurtured "awareness" confidence and enhanced individual uniqueness
- Cultivated visual thinking
- Stimulated unique insights, thoughts, and answers
- Fostered an innovation culture
- Enhanced creative capacity to unlock ideas and concepts
- Improved flexible thought
- Improved performance, efficiency, and productivity
- Developed influencing skills to turn ideas into action and get results
- Improved communication skills and strong listening skills
- Stepped outside of the comfort zone
- Achieved leadership development, accountability, and responsibility
- Helped students to identify and correct weaknesses
- Helped students to think on a "manager level" to learn to link their competencies to the overall team's performance
- Learned to work effectively as a team
- Faced problems head-on
- Stimulated vision, and /or identified self-values
- Overcame many fears of leadership *with its* responsibility/accountability
- Enhanced presentation skills
- Encourage *collaborative leadership*
- Engaged the unexpected with clarity, courage and mental agility
- Took pride of ownership and built confidence
- Developed a heightened sense of creativity, imagination and innovative "thought" that could be applied immediately to daily tasks
- Gained clearer sense of value to one's self, one's skills and to teammates
- Achieved resourcefulness, ingenuity, and enterprise
- Increased initiative and problem-solving ability, especially in difficult situations
- Connected to the lessons of the past to ensure that everyone knows where they have been, what they are up against, and their plan for tomorrow
- Opened up to change

- Asked solution based questions
- Tried new things
- Took calculated risks
- Learned to find more in-depth purpose in connection with the tasks at hand
- Stepped up to challenges and gave their all
- Enhanced their intuition

How many business executives or entrepreneurs would love to have employees like this? Also, these newly discovered skills and enhanced abilities will serve these students throughout their entire lives if they choose to use them consistently.

Therefore, even if you are one of the head honchos at Amazon, you are going to take from this book at least one new success quality, strategy or principle that will add to your already fantastic repertoire of success. You may gain an edge that will surge you ahead of the pack, and gain greater insight into what makes you tick, and how you can achieve even greater success.

What's So Special About You?

WHAT CAN ANYONE WHO WANTS TO BE HAPPY AND SUCCESSFUL LEARN FROM THIS BOOK?

Well, since you are reading this book, I believe that you are looking for something greater in yourself and your life. You most likely want to be 'rich' and have financial independence, feel secure in your own future, and live a fabulous life. But what that translates into is this: You need to learn *how to separate yourself from the competition, to realize your true potential, and learn how to offer up your personal best in everything you do. Or look at it this way, learn to be unique, find your passion and get out there!*

When you, the reader, continue to take yourself *diligently* through the reading of this book and take on the challenges of empowering yourself to new heights, you will find that you too can easily use these success qualities to your benefit for quick life-changing results. What you will learn in this book *is all relative to you and your success.*

For example, DeVry University released its annual "Job Preparedness Indicator." This survey is designed to measure the disparity between candidate skills and employer expectations. Interestingly, the top attributes that employers are looking to see demonstrated in candidate resumes are:

- Ability to work in a team
- Leadership
- Communication skills (written)
- Problem-solving skills
- Strong work ethic
- Motivation/Initiative

In addition, here are the most important candidate *skills/abilities* that *Job Outlook* survey says employers are looking for in their potential hires:

- Ability to work in a team structure
- Ability to lead
- Ability to verbally communicate
- Strong work ethic
- Ability to make decisions and solve problems
- Ability to obtain and process information

What's So Special About You?

- Ability to plan, organize and prioritize work
- Ability to sell or influence others
- Ability to show initiative
- Honesty & Integrity

Same with the National Association of Colleges and Employers (NACE) say the top skills employers are seeking are the following:

- Ability to verbally communicate
- Ability to work in a team structure
- Strong work ethic
- Ability to lead
- Ability to obtain and process information
- Ability to make decisions and solve problems

It's the same attributes shuffled around showing the same success message again, and the top business leaders know this.

Surveys the world over are very similar to what is wanted and in every job or career.

Ultimately, the mission of this book is to help you discover success qualities, boost your natural strengths, overcome weaknesses and fears, and enhance your abilities by synergizing the successful character qualities of the world's most successful people.

You are going to learn how to be an agent of change, pursue vision, take calculated risks, think and act differently from others, gain a higher social intelligence, connect deeply with anyone, have true persuasive communication power, be willing to take the lead, be able to love yourself enough to fail *and learn from the experience*, make an amazing impression on others, and know that you can change your world or "the world" on a small or large scale. *Where you can step into your chosen field ready to offer excellence, feed your soul and achieve happiness.*

Thus, the opportunity for you to live your dreams has never been as great as this moment in history. More than ever, people everywhere are searching for opportunities to create happiness and wealth. I hope YOU are one of them because your answers are right here.

What's So Special About You?

SELF ASSESSMENT CHALLENGE
HOW DO YOU RATE WITH THE BEST?

In my research of the world's most successful people, I have found that they embrace 77 personality traits or winning qualities which they live by.

It is these 77 qualities that encompass and radiate their personal lifestyle. Their success and happiness is an extension of their lives, and it is these 77 empowering qualities that make all the difference between them and everyone else.

Now, if a "regular" person was to embrace just 1 of these 77 qualities and make the conscious effort to use it in their daily life, then what would happen? Well, you would alter the course of your life by a simple degree. That 1 degree of change would over time, alter your life significantly and in so many unimaginable ways. That's the power of this work.

Photo Credit: Claus Anderson

For example one of my clients, Mark McKoy, is the retired Canadian track and field winner of the Gold Medal for 110 meters' hurdles at the 1992 Summer Olympics. Mark told me a fascinating story of what helped him win the gold medal. He had competed in a couple of Olympics before, only to make fourth place at best.

What's So Special About You?

His last attempt to win gold was in Barcelona in 1992. He was 31 years old, considered by many as "over the hill," and he was up against athletes much younger than himself. Mark was teased by many as being the "Fourth place winner'. In their eyes, McKoy was not considered a real threat.

So Mark told me his life-changing story, where a few months earlier he had traveled to England and met a coach who worked with him. The coach had Mark run his typical 110 meters hurdle race. Within minutes, the coach could see that when Mark was running, he would land his left foot onto the surface at a wide angle, losing an inch in his stride. So the coach suggested that he angle his foot more inwards in line with his forward lunge.

Photo Credit: Claus Anderson

This slight degree change added an extra inch to each of his 39 steps in the race. Mark spectacularly won in the Summer Olympics in Barcelona, Spain, 1992, taking the Gold Medal in the 110m hurdles.

It was the first Track Gold Medal for Canada in 64 years! He passed the finish line 39 inches ahead of the second place winner! Mark said it was that "one inch of change that transformed the course of his life forever." Today, Mark is a very successful personal fitness trainer and guest speaker, who travels the world inspiring people everywhere.

Mark McKoy's "one inch of change" is the same transformational idea as making a "1 degree" directional change to your life by embracing at least one of the 77 success qualities presented here in this book.

What's So Special About You?

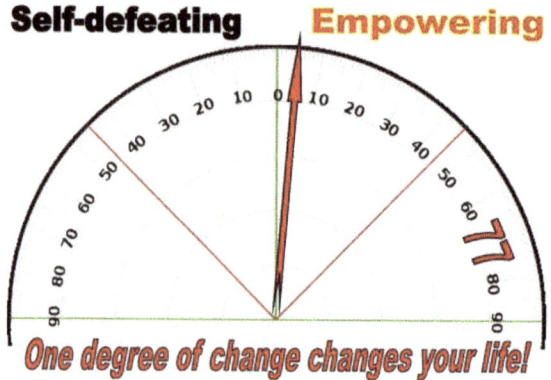

Many of these qualities you may already have, but just imagine what would happen if you were to make a 5 or 10-degree change to your life? What would happen if you were to embrace all 77 degrees of change fearlessly?

I'll tell you what would happen, your life would be transformed as you could never imagine. Your actions would rock your world; doors would open, new opportunities would become available, and a whole new lifestyle would manifest; a new inspiring lifestyle that never would have happened if you had not made the changes needed. Perhaps for you, it's time to begin the process of change to a new lifestyle of happiness and success.

What's So Special About You?

The 77 empowering qualities are broken down by chapter: each chapter contains 7 or 8. Rate yourself honestly and see how you compare with the world's most successful people. The scale is 5 (self-defeating) to 1 (Empowering).

Now, remember, what you "agree" to and what you actually do may be two different things, so be thoughtful and truthful with yourself when answering the questions, and take your time.

Your answers will show you where you share similar thoughts, beliefs, and where you take actions just like "successful people."

However, more importantly, your answers also reveal what you need to improve on and make adjustments. You want to transform your self-defeating or average habits and beliefs up so that you are feeling empowered, and then miracles will happen.

And just how do you convert your self-defeating actions into high empowerment positions you might ask? Well, let's say you are in the self-defeating position when it comes to having the "courage" to speak to a crowd of people, as most people are. What you need to do is take the actions needed to change your position from low to high. So let's say you start by offering to speak at your friend's wedding or birthday, and even though it was hard doing it, you still did it. You spoke in public - congratulations!

Speaking in public is a good start because you have proved that you can do it. You feel inspired and even empowered, but those feelings will only last a short time.

What's So Special About You?

So while you're feeling courageous, you now take it to the next level. Push yourself to take more deliberate and specific actions that challenge your courage. You might join Toastmasters or take an acting improvisation class to help you. Whatever you decide to do, you want to challenge yourself to improve. You MUST engage yourself to take the appropriate actions until you feel that being courageous is a part of your new lifestyle. Therefore, the bottom line is this: *be consistent with your positive actions in order to move yourself into feeling empowered.*

In the final chapter of this book, the last round of success qualities will be revealed so you can add up your overall total score, and see how you rate with the best in the world.

I know that going through the list of 77 winning qualities may become "overwhelming." But, I shall make no apologies for the effort required. Instead, I suggest you get excited at the 77 opportunities to make real improvements in your life. So digest the information and be truthful with yourself and YOU will be setting yourself up for success by design!

What's So Special About You?

77 QUALITIES ONLINE COURSE

Welcome to the

77 WINNING LIFESTYLE FORMULA COURSE

You receive the Book, 10 set Online Course and the e-Book.

If you feel inspired, you can always access the actual "non-acting" part of the course online, and from which this book was created.

In the **77 Qualities Online Course** that runs for 10 weeks, you will learn how to ***apply*** the 77 qualities from the worlds most successful people ***consistently*** and you will thrive!

When you finish a chapter in the book, visit www.77GlobalVillage.com for a more in-depth journey into the book subject's corresponding chapter, where I will take you through the steps that will help you move your life along on the path of the world's most successful people.

I shall encourage you to review the success qualities for that chapter and to take one of your weakest qualities through the actions needed to move it into one of your empowering success qualities.

Your home study assignments will also consist of writing in your journal and doing exercises to help you step into the shoes of the world's most successful people and be the best you can be. It's important that you engage in the exercises provided because it's in the *"doing"* that you will experience the reality of empowerment.

What's So Special About You?

Also with the online course, I include my *"Game changer"* tips. Now, based on in-depth research, if you were to do just the game changer tips and nothing else, then you would still significantly increase the success in your life.

FYI ~ when you purchase my **77 Qualities Online Course** I will reward you with the final work in this series, **"What's So Special About US?"**.

This eBook constitutes the *"Crown Jewels"* to all my year's research into the world's most successful people and will be yours, free.

This eBook reveals insights and teachings for anyone wanting to learn how best to empower themselves so they can do their part in helping change the world. I also show what I consider truly unique, which are the *"Three human achievements"* needed to become an iconic trailblazer on the world's stage, along with **five core founding principles of all success and transcendence** with a seriously life-changing, in-depth insight into each of them.

Finally, I reveal my original image of the powerful *"Transcendence Crest,"* that manifested from my dream, which you can use daily to change your life, each day! Discover the magic of *what's so special about us* and be guided to happiness, success, and *transcendence*. And best of all, it's free to you as my way of saying thank you when you purchase my online course. So, please visit

www.77GlobalVillage.com

Also, when you get a moment, please check out my new video show ***Frequency of Success*** at
www.77GlobalVillage.com

What's So Special About You?

Finally, and in the words of one of my students Arielle from her journal…

~ "We all have the capability to do great things" ~

"Today we talked about guiding our own ship, and about being in charge of our own careers and of our own choices. How many people never realize the potential they have, they just go with the flow and hope it takes them to where they want to be. They don't put in the effort because they are too lazy or they just don't know how.

Mr. Healy has taught us that we have to be more than just actors; we need to be entrepreneurs, in business for ourselves. It's not about thinking outside the box; it's about living there. Because we all have the capability to do great things, we just needed a little perspective and guidance, and the way they were given to us was truly unique.

We weren't taught how to be great; we were shown that we already are great. We weren't forced to change but encouraged to grow. We were given the opportunity to become better people, and that is a lesson that goes beyond this course. It's a lesson that lasts a lifetime. The journey I went through has been documented in these journals, and I can say without a doubt that I have changed. By reading this book, you will have changed. What will set you apart is, either changing because you have to or learning to change because you want to".

-Arielle a student from the course.

What's So Special About You?

I do believe that it would be a safe bet to say that there must be tens of thousands of books written on the topics of self-improvement in one form or another, and perhaps millions of articles written that overlap in every conceivable area of self-improvement, business strategy, leadership and how to be successful, blah, blah, blah.

So when I decided to take on the massive responsibility of actually writing this book, I knew that I was not an "expert" in any of the above fields.

However, I am a learned man, with sharp and keen insight, a nose for detailed research, an intuition that guides me daily, and I knew that my approach would be somewhat *out-of-the-box*, definitive and results-driven.

Are you ready?

Let's begin.

> **"The old believe everything; the middle-aged suspect everything, the young know everything."**
>
> - Oscar Wilde

What's So Special About You?

KNOW THYSELF
(Chapter 1 – Week 1)

"I hope everyone that is reading this is having a really good day. And if not, just know that in every new minute that passes you have an opportunity to change that."

(Gillian Anderson. Scully in the X-Files.)

If you want to achieve your life's dream and be successful, you need to model yourself after people who are already living their dreams.
The more qualities you have in common with the world's most successful people, the higher your chances for being successful.

Acting allows us to overcome fears and anxieties, to communicate, play and think outside the box, around the box, and through the box in an imaginative, fun and free-flowing manner. To be an actor or entrepreneur or a business leader is to be a risk taker, creative, courageous, resourceful and innovative. This means to have the capacity to think freely, openly, without limitations or constraints about problems and challenges.

When we think freely, we are creative; we tend to see opportunities and possibilities that we would usually filter out of our personal experience because most people get stuck on the 'limitations" or become lost and overwhelmed by the problems. We need to separate ourselves from this self-defeating reality and adopt a new reality in the footsteps of the world's most successful people.

Chapter 1 ~ Know Thyself

SO WHAT IS SUCCESS?

How would you like to grow yourself into a living, breathing, reality? Where you are able to inspire others and become just like the world's most successful people? Where you believe, beyond all doubt, that your life can be unique and successful?

Would you love to live a life as cherished as that?

So then, I will ask you this, what does success mean to you?

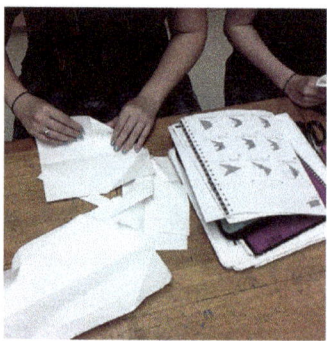

If you don't know how to define success for yourself, then how can you create it? How can you build a simple toy, paper-airplane if you don't see the steps involved? What would the finished product look like? How would it fly? The truth is, you can't unless you're prepared to try every conceivable way, test each result, and then go back to the drawing board and try again, and again, and again.

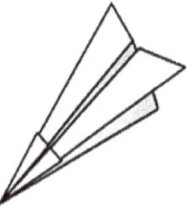

The same truth applies to success. However, you don't need to go to the drawing board to hammer out success, because success already has a blueprint that you can follow, and has been proven tens of thousands of times throughout history by the world's most successful people.

What's So Special About You?

Truth is, most people are stumbling over each other in hot pursuit of "success." They want the money, cars, fame, wealth, houses, around the world adventures, the latest gadgets, hot women, sexy men, you name it, and they want it! Moreover, we see generalized "success" as being the means to achieving it all... Maybe yes, but then again, maybe not. The definition of success is subjective. My definition might be different than yours.

I read a book titled 'Man's Search for Meaning' by Viktor E Frank, a man who survived five years in Nazi death camps and he would tell you; *"Don't aim at success. The more you aim at it and make it a target, the more you are going to miss it. For success, like happiness, cannot be pursued; it must ensue, and it only does so as the unintended side-effect of one's personal dedication to a cause greater than oneself or as the by-product of one's surrender to a person other than oneself. Happiness must happen, and the same holds for success: you have to let it happen by not caring about it. I want you to listen to what your conscience commands you to do and go on to carry it out to the best of your knowledge. Then you will live to see that in the long-run—in the long-run, I say!—success will follow you precisely because you had forgotten to think about it."*

So how do you define success? Your success?

- having lots of money
- being happy in your efforts at work and play with family and friends
- making progress in your life
- winning the deal, the game, winning in the trading, winning the girl. WIN! WIN! WIN!
- giving your best efforts
- feeling successful by working in harmony with other like-minded individuals
- having balance in your life
- leaving a positive legacy after your death
- making a positive difference in people's lives
- not being a quitter
- growing on a personal level
- realizing your dreams
- achieving your goals
- feeling secure
- having peace of mind

Chapter 1 ~ Know Thyself

- having health and vitality (what's the point of having all the money if your health is gone?)
- having a loving family

Your definition of success depends on the meaning you give to the success you seek. Ask yourself, *what is my purpose?* Why do I want to be successful? Ask yourself, what does success mean to me?

In the insightful words of one of America's most successful women, Arianna Huffington - *"Life is shaped from the inside out, not the outside in."*

So many people believe that success is about having lots of money and things, but the truth is that the reel feeling of success lies within how you see yourself and how you're able to enjoy your life, regardless if you are rich or poor.

I know a successful man named Troy Skog, who had his own concept of success, then one day he walked away from his ranch with over 15 horses. He let go of all the stuff he had acquired and went walkabout into the jungles of Ecuador for five months. All he had was a pack on his back with a few personal items. He had very little money. No credit cards. Couldn't speak the language, and he had no idea of where he was going. He was a man unprepared for the jungle, but that did not stop him. He had no idea where he would get a meal from or how he would survive. He just knew that he would be okay.

He trusted his intuition, and so this white man with a cowboy hat walked from village to village. He met local villagers who would offer him food, and in return, he would dig them water wells, or help build a schoolhouse, or fix something that needed fixing. When he came out of the jungle, he told me the most inspiring stories of how he met so many amazing people, helped kids by building a medical center, drilled wells, fixed huts, and he never went a day without having a meal - for five months!

You can bet his concept of success has changed. His life has changed. He came out happier and more fulfilled than when he first went into the Jungle. Everyone said he was crazy before he left, but he knew that he would be okay, and for five months, he lived an entirely successful life without a penny and had a Jungle adventure, most of us can only dream about. He is now writing a book about his inspiring journey into the unknown.

Would you do it? Leave everything behind and "go bush" for a while?

Throughout all my years of research into the world's most successful people, I believe being successful is about following your heart, listening to your gut, and giving this "life" your best and most enthusiastic efforts, all the while trusting that you'll attract what you need, and you'll attract what you want, and you'll "tune-in" to life's meaning along the way. Whether you tune-in to *all* that is offered or *all* that is presented to you along the journey is another question. Ultimately, though, being successful is about choosing to be the best you can be, making a positive difference in people's lives and living your life with purpose.

Finally, on helping you define or review success for yourself, I would like to quote the American poet, Ralph Waldo Emerson. *"To laugh often and much: To win the respect of intelligent people and the affection of children, to earn the appreciation of honest critics and endure the betrayal of false friends; to appreciate beauty, to find the best in others, to leave the world a bit better whether by a healthy child, a garden patch, or a redeemed social condition; to know even one life has breathed easier because you lived. This is to have succeeded."*

In the photo, Troy is on the right with a Mayan shaman named Pablo, and a 72 yr old rainbow child hippie. All three met each other while on their own jungle journeys. Together they built an outdoor kitchen to feed 50 orphan kids a day in a small town called San Pablo and then went their separate ways to continue their journeys. *Beautiful!*

Chapter 1 ~ Know Thyself

Troy returned to Canada to run a successful Yoga business.

So, what does success mean to you? Let that question ferment for a while as you continue to read on.

If you want to achieve your life's dream and be successful, you need to model yourself after people who are already living their dreams.

The more qualities you have in common with the world's most successful people, the higher your chances of being successful.

Your goal in this first chapter is to get a clear picture of yourself, complete with all the flaws, and then you can begin the renovations from within.

Changing the world is what the world's most successful people can do, and you can be just as successful if you learn from them, make the changes needed and position yourself accordingly. The "magic bullet" is what the Bible tells us - *"Know thyself."*

Because knowing *What's so special about* YOU and what's so special about the world's most successful people can and will make you happier and wealthier!

> **"Those who cannot change their minds cannot change anything."**
> George Bernard Shaw

Your success or failure is first based on how you think. Remember that, for *how you think determines your destiny*. And if you have doubts about that, then this is why YOU are in the camp of the other 90%.

Take a moment here to consider what you've been thinking about recently. For example, have you been feeling positive or negative? Do you have a negative outlook on life in general or a more positive outlook?

This is critical because it comes down to what you have been telling yourself? Are you telling yourself that you have had a shitty year so far? Or, that you are always struggling? Or are you having thoughts that you just can't seem to cope, or that you are a loser and your overall feeling is just negative, negative, negative?

Or are you, for the most part, feeling upbeat and positive with your life? Are you telling yourself nurturing thoughts that elevate your spirits and make you feel good?

I bring all this up at this time because I want you to be aware of your thoughts, because "thoughts" affect your habits and behaviors. So start by taking stock of the dominant thoughts running through your mind. Are you happy or unhappy person?

Over twenty-five years of teaching and studying the successful qualities of the world's most successful people, I have discovered time and time again that these successful people do not think and act the same as everyone else. In fact, as you will soon discover, they have character qualities, success strategies and disciplines that they live by, which truly separates them from the world's other 90 percent, who are just regular people; otherwise known as mediocre, commonplace, ordinary or as they believe, "nothing special."

Are these "successful people" smarter than the rest of us? Not really. Are they luckier? No, and they are certainly not perfect by any stretch of the imagination. In fact, many were born into poverty, broken families and yes, they all had many personal issues – just like all of us.

However, they do think differently from everybody else, and as a result, they act differently.

Try answering these simple questions below, along with all the questions throughout this book, because your answers will define your failures and your successes.

Is the glass half empty or half-full?

Are you a pessimist, worrywart, complainer, nit-pickier, whiner, always blame, blame, blame, excuses, excuses and more excuses, or are you an optimist, someone who aspires to, or abides by high standards or principles?

Chapter 1 ~ Know Thyself

Are you someone who takes responsibility, is inspiring, hard-working, applies self-discipline, walks through the fires of life and through the inner fears, who overcome procrastination and rejects internal resistance? OR are someone who is lazy, shuns responsibility, has no backbone for self-discipline, doesn't give a shit about others but only pretends too to get money or better your lot in life?

Just by reading the above descriptions, you can quickly work out who is on track to success and who is in serious trouble. Which are you? Or, what parts of the above descriptions are most like you?

Thinking positive doesn't solve the world's problems, but it sure beats thinking negative. Thinking positive allows you to at least be open to progressive possibilities while thinking negative shuts those possibilities down. In other words, you limit yourself.

Most people have a level of thinking that limits their belief in themselves and prevents them from becoming truly successful in Life. For example, review this interesting information below, and ask yourself what mindset do you have?

PEOPLE WITH A MINDSET OF ABUNDANCE ARE GENERALLY:

- Confident
- Grounded
- Have a sense of gratitude
- Like reading
- Share their ideas
- Like to participate
- Are happy people
- Forgive others and move on
- Accept responsibilities for their own mistakes
- Genuinely want others to succeed
- Are goal oriented
- Always learning new things
- Keep a to do list

What's So Special About You?

PEOPLE WITH A MINDSET OF SCARCITY ARE GENERALLY:

- Having a chip on their shoulder
- Unforgiving
- Unproductive most of the time
- Non-participating
- Blaming, whining, complaining and bitching
- Thinking they know everything
- Prone to hostility
- Not goal setters
- Unreliable
- Two faced
- Untrustworthy
- Flying by the seat of their pants
- Not sharing
- Fearing change
- Taking credit for as much as they can
- All about me, me, me!

I would like you to answer the questions on the following page using the scale of #1 on the left = you ALMOST NEVER, or to the #5 position on the right, meaning ALMOST ALWAYS consistently. #2, 3, 4 are between the two extremes.

Which ones do you apply/agree with that you rate highly on; and where do you rate low? Your answers will show where you need to improve. Take your time with this and be truthful with yourself because success starts with the truth! If you are reading an e-Book, then you can go to my site and download a print off to use.

www.77GlobalVillage.com

Chapter 1 ~ Know Thyself

Unsuccessful people tend to be or have:

| | | | | Worrying constantly (scale of 1 almost never to 5 almost always) |

| | | | | Thinking small |

| | | | | Following along with the crowd |

| | | | | Habit of procrastination |

| | | | | Habit of perfectionism |

| | | | | Limiting or holding you back beliefs, emotions and attitudes |

| | | | | Fear of failure |

| | | | | Fear of taking risks |

| | | | | Inability to listen to instructions carefully |

What's So Special About You?

					Inability to plan ahead

					Inability to say "no" to others

					Inability to consider the consequences of our actions

					Inability to think flexibly about problems

					Inability to admit mistakes

					Have unrealistic expectations

					Critically judging self

					Critically judging others

					Constantly comparing self to others

					Always complaining about people, circumstances or bad luck

					Limiting thoughts focused on what's not working or on unrealistic daydreams

Below are words self-defeating or "average" people use to stop themselves from moving forward into uncharted waters. Please use the scale of **#1 on left meaning you ALMOST NEVER use the term or the #5 on the right meaning you ALMOST ALWAYS consistently use the term, which is self-defeating.** How often do you say or think the words below?

37

Chapter 1 ~ Know Thyself

				I can't do it (meaning you won't)

				This won't work

				It's just not fair

				That never happens to me

				Why can't that ever happen to me?

				I hate doing this

				I'm too busy (being thrown out there to deliberately avoid)

				I'm not ready yet (just stalling)

				I'm not good enough

				I don't have the confidence

				I hate how I...

				I can't because...

				Yeah-but
				I knew (something negative about you) that was going to happen
				I'll try but I don't know
				But I'm shy
				I hate going first
				I wish I were like him/her

WHAT IS YOUR FINAL SCORE? Tally up all 38 questions and give yourself a score of 1, 2, 3, 4 or 5 for each tick you placed in the appropriate box as shown below.

SCORES =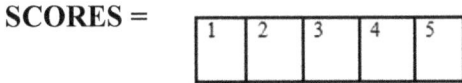

If you ticked all the boxes going down the LEFT SIDE of the page, your score would be 38 which is excellent. You are in the right frame of mind, and as such, you are on the path towards happiness and success. Anything more than 38 and you're holding yourself back more and more as the score gets higher. You want the score to be as LOW as possible to 38, which sets you on the right mental path to happiness and success.

If you were honest in your ratings to all 38 questions above, then you can now see where you lack, and how you're holding yourself back. Look at the ratings in detail for it reveals your weaknesses thus far, and yes, we will be digging a lot deeper as we go so be advised. The good news here is that you now know a part of what's holding you back from success, and you now know some of the areas you need to focus on for improvement. Let me say, though, that this new discovery of self-learning is just the beginning.

Chapter 1 ~ Know Thyself

OUR FIRST WEEK IN CLASS

On day one of the first week, I jokingly introduced myself as the "Village idiot" to the 12 students, all complete strangers sitting before me. They went stone-faced. I could see them mentally trying to work out in their heads my "village idiot" remark and what I could have possibly meant by saying it.

I told the students that this first week would be an introduction, where they will learn about me, my rules and my teaching concepts. They will also learn about each other as classmates, their environment and also begin to learn about themselves.

The students themselves came into my course from all walks of life and countries. They all sat in their chairs, feeling a little anxious. Some made friends quickly, with smiles and handshakes, while others were less sure. All had their expectations of what the acting course was going to be like, but none could have imagined what it was really going to be like.

I remember looking at each of them, looking back at me. They all had their masks on, the masks they wanted others to see. They were young, inexperienced and filled with hope, untapped potential, and talent. But talent is what you start with.

What all of them were going to need to get through this course in one triumphant piece, was the *courage* to open up their minds and to freely see and feel what they were actually capable of.

The first lesson for them to learn and agree to was that I wanted a *commitment from each of them, that no matter what, (unless sick with a doctor's note) that each one of them would arrive each and every morning on time with their work fully prepared and ready to begin.* I mean, how else are they even going to get a shot at living their dreams if they are not willing to do what is expected of any leading player or even a manager – *turn up on time ready to work.*

They all agreed.

The second lesson to learn was to unlearn what you think you know, and that begins with willingly giving up your sense of "control."

What's So Special About You?

You see, people don't like to give up control. It's like trying to persuade a cat not to be afraid of the bath water. It can be done, but it does meet with heavy resistance.

With that said let's see how you face your inner resistance when you begin the 1st self-assessment of ten rounds.

Begin on the next page.

Chapter 1 ~ Know Thyself

YOUR ASSESSMENT CHALLENGE

Below is the first round of my success by design self-assessment challenge. Review these character traits/beliefs and honestly rate yourself on a scale of the box on the left means you use it ALMOST ALWAYS, or you DO believe it. The box on the right position means you ALMOST NEVER use it or DON'T believe it. So #1 is empowering, and #5 is self-defeating, and #3 is halfway.

1	2	3	4	5

HOW DO YOU RATE WITH THE BEST - ROUND 1

Successful people tend to be or have:

1/Humility: They have a strength within themselves that says, I don't need to show off. In fact, Sir Isaac Newton said it well, *"If I have seen further than others; it is by standing on the shoulders of giants."* Or as the academic and novelist C. S. Lewis once remarked *"Humanity is not thinking less of yourself, but thinking of yourself less."* [So, the question is how humble are you?]

2/Optimistic Attitude: The world's most successful people stay optimistic and positive. They understand that being mentally in a positive state of mind is a positive mindset to have is the sharp edge between failure and success. [On what scale do you have an optimistic attitude?]

3/Belief: Successful people really do believe in themselves. Never underestimate what you can achieve when you believe in yourself. To be clear, belief is NOT self-confidence. For example, you can believe in yourself as a person who will rise above challenges; however, you may lack the confidence to jump out of an airplane on your first lesson, until you gain the confidence. [How much do you truly believe in you as a person who can rise above adversity?]

What's So Special About You?

☐☐☐☐☐ **4/Visualize:** They dream big and create exciting visuals of what their success looks and feels like, and they live in the vibrational energy of that success. They don't wait to be successful for they live it now. They know that they are successful now in the moment, and have gratitude for it now. Vision boards are a great idea. [Do you create visuals of success for yourself?]

☐☐☐☐☐ **5/Inspiring:** They possess free-flowing energy that often inspires others to achieve higher ambitions. They inspire others to find their "inner voice" or inner genius. [Very special question here – On what scale do you inspire others to find their inner voice?]

☐☐☐☐☐ **6/Love:** The world's most successful people apply the power of love in all that they do because what they do feeds their soul and they make a living from it. They love life, family, friends, good times, business, peace, prosperity, inspiring others to greatness and making a difference in the world. Everyone else works for a living and saves what they love to do for some other time. [On what scale does the work that you do feed your soul?]

☐☐☐☐☐ **7/Learn:** They are always open to learning new things, new experiences, learning about the world around them and what they need to learn to advance forward. [How open are you to learning new things?]

☐☐☐☐☐ **8/Discerning:** *To perceive, recognize, or comprehend with the mind; to catch sight of something difficult to discern.* The world's most successful people have good judgment. They are able to discern truth from error. They are able to understand people, things, and situations clearly and intelligently. [On what scale can you discern?]

What's your score for round 1?

Chapter 1 ~ Know Thyself

From the total of 8 questions, tally up and give yourself a 1, 2, 3, 4, or 5 for each tick you placed in the appropriate box as below.

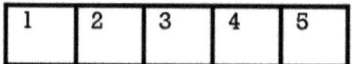

Best score is 8, and the worst score is 40. Look at your results and compare with the world's most successful people. Can you see where you are on par with them and where you need improvement?

Okay so my question to you is, what are you going to do about the improvements you need to make to better yourself? Pick one of them right now.

Go ahead, I'll wait...

Okay, you have picked one quality that needs improvement. So how are you going to challenge yourself to a higher empowering level with that quality that needs improvement?

What are you going to do about it and when do you begin?

Get a pen and write below the line what you are going to do and when you are going to do it.

Now make it an agreement with yourself. Make it a promise. Set a deadline now and live up to it.

Go ahead. I'll wait.

What's So Special About You?

Now, I know some people would advise you not to worry about your weaknesses and focus only on your strengths.

However, if your weaknesses are holding you back, then it won't matter what strengths you think you have, because if your foundation is weak at the core, then you're going to lose!

Besides, what military commander would say to his men, "Forget about your weaknesses?" Oh, really? I don't think so! So stop going off half-cocked and get your weaknesses up to empowering levels and see the massive improvement to your achievement abilities then. Read the quote below and embrace it as your new gospel.

> **"Thoughts lead on to purposes; purposes go forth in action; actions form habits; habits decide character, and character fixes our destiny."**
>
> - Tryon Edwards

To achieve success means: you need to "think" in a way that produces the best results every time. It means that your thinking must be on a higher level of self-awareness and then your chances of producing the best results are greatly improved.

Now, if thinking positive like *"I can"* sounds just like *"new age thinking,"* then you might like to know that people who believe in themselves live longer, healthier lives, and have more financial wealth than all those people that keep thinking they *"can't."*

Besides, successful people actively work on taking risks, stretching themselves beyond their comfort levels, and work hard to gain the confidence, experience, and competence needed to overcome their inner fears, master new things and get results.

In other words, *they become confident by challenging themselves*, and they *choose* to believe and have faith in their ability to overcome all obstacles. So, begin your path to success by unlearning what you have learned and change your mindset.

Chapter 1 ~ Know Thyself

THE POWER OF VISUALIZATION
("What dark wizardry be this?")

No its truly not any type of wizardry but it is super powerful. Here is the first big realization for you to grasp if you haven't done it already in your life. The world's most successful people visualize their results in advance of achieving them, and they have a powerful purpose that drives them through all barriers. For example each day in my acting class we would gather at the same time, 10:30 am and begin with deep breathing exercises to align our minds and bodies to the natural rhythms within ourselves. Then I would take the students on a three-minute visualization, where I would have them visualize what success looked like to them, and how that "success" felt. I encouraged the students to visualize their "success" to the point that they felt excited. That's the emotion we want to feel – excitement!

They could visualize anything as long as it was at the end of their journey. What would one moment in one day of your success look like, whatever that "success" means to you? What would it feel like? Are you driving a sports car in the Alps? Are you sipping your favorite drink in your seaside home? What are you doing?

The reality is that the world's most successful people from Steve Jobs to Oprah to Muhammad Ali, to Arnold Schwarzenegger, and the success list goes on to include all the world's top movers and shakers in business, sports, or any other profession you would like to mention, all *know the importance of starting with the end in mind, and they get very excited about the end of the journey…first.* They take the time to actually picture it to themselves in detail, succeeding in their mind's eye before they actually succeed in their reality.

Here's how it works. First, when most people think of a goal or a dream, it's usually limited to their own world of beliefs and understandings. Seldom do people think outside of their own world or their own mental sandbox.

Next, when most regular people really want to achieve something; they first start out all inspired and motivated. Then they begin second-guessing, listening to the naysayers, over analyzing it and allowing all "real world realities" or obstacles to drag them down into the drudgery of mediocrity. Before they know it, they are distracted once again and running on autopilot, while their dream fades away.

Others may get past the thinking stage and actually get working on their dream only to give up when their journey turns from the "path of least resistance" into a struggle.

Now, by contrast, let's look at people like Jim Carrey, who when in the early nineties was a completely unknown actor living in a Camper Van with his Parents and family. Then he wrote himself a Cheque for $10 million, and he also wrote on the cheque - for "*Acting services rendered,*" and then he dated it 1994. He carried this cheque in his wallet for inspiration because he really wanted to change his reality. Then when he made the film Dumb and Dumber, he was paid $10 million. The rest is movie star history.

Or how about this guy named David Seidler.

Can you imagine cancer away?
By Elizabeth Cohen, CNN Senior Medical Correspondent

David Seidler won an Oscar for best original screenplay for "The King's Speech," was a stutterer just like King George VI, whose battle with the speech disorder is portrayed in the film. What you might not know is that Seidler, 73, suffered from cancer, just like the king did. But unlike his majesty, Seidler survived cancer, and he says he did so because **he used the same vivid imagination he employed to write his award-winning script.**

Seidler says **he visualized his cancer away.** "I know it sounds awfully Southern California and woo-woo," he admits when he describes the visualization techniques he used when his bladder cancer was diagnosed nearly six years ago. "But that's what happened."

Seidler says when he found out his cancer had returned, he visualized a "lovely, clean, healthy bladder" for two weeks, and the cancer disappeared. He's been cancer-free for more than five years.

Whether you can imagine away cancer or any other disease, has been hotly debated for years. One camp of doctors will tell you that they've seen patients do it and that a whole host of studies supports the mind-

Chapter 1 ~ Know Thyself

body connection. Other doctors, just as well respected, will tell you the notion is preposterous, and there's not a single study to prove it really works.

Seidler isn't concerned about studies. He says all he knows is that for him, visualization worked.

"When I was first diagnosed in 2005, I was rather upset, of course," Seidler says in a telephone interview from his home in Malibu, California. "After three to four days of producing a lot of mucus and salty tears, I knew prolonged grief was bad for the autoimmune system, and the autoimmune system was the only buddy I had in fighting cancer."

"I spent hours visualizing a nice, cream-colored unblemished bladder lining, and then I went in for the operation, and a week later the doctor called me, and his voice was very strange," Seidler remembers. "He said, 'I don't know how to explain it, but there's no cancer there.' He says the doctor was so confounded he sent the tissue from the presurgical biopsy to four different labs, and all confirmed they were cancerous. The mind does have the power to heal.

He says he believes the supplements and visualizations were behind what his doctor called a "spontaneous remission" -- plus a change in his way of thinking. He stopped feeling sorry for himself because of his cancer and his impending divorce.

"I was very grief-stricken," he remembers. "It was a 30-year marriage, and in my grief, I could tell I was getting sicker. I decided to just change my head around."

While Seidler says he knows his unorthodox recovery techniques sound "woo-woo" to some ears, they sound "like science" to **Dr. Christiane Northrup,** a best-selling author who's written extensively on the mind-body connection. "This doesn't sound woo-woo to me," she says. "The mind has the power to heal."

To read the full article go to
http://www.cnn.com/2011/HEALTH/03/03/ep.seidler.cancer.mind.body/

What's So Special About You?

So, when you begin the daily ritual of taking ten minutes a day to disconnect from all that's around you. Just breathe it all away. Then when you begin using your imagination to see/feel/believe yourself like you are in a movie working your success or enjoying your success - *life changes*.

The more vivid you can get, the better it will work for you. Remember, the little details increase the likelihood of your big picture actually happening over time. For example, Muhammad Ali, three-time heavyweight boxing Champion of the world, once said he would visualize round by round, every detail in the ring with his opponent weeks and sometimes months before a fight.

Be specific and use visualization every day as part of your overall plan/campaign for achieving your goals. Use it every day, and you will greatly increase the odds in your favor. Now, do you have to take the natural step-by-step process in getting what you want and work hard and smart at the same time? I would say in 99% of cases YES!

In fact, use as many of the 77 winning qualities as you can, and you are going to launch yourself into the stratosphere. In other words, you will generate a *vortex of success* around yourself like you could never have imagined before. Now, let's be clear, it's not wizardry or magic. It's not a trick. It's not supernatural. It's not daydreaming. It's not wishful thinking. It's not entertaining fantasy, and it's not hoping for the best. Having said that, this is what Oprah Winfrey tells us *"Create the highest, grandest vision possible for your life because you become what you believe."*

So to do what Oprah is suggesting you do, you must first *open your mind* to go beyond what you already know now, and "think" yourself way beyond your own "outer limits" and into another world of make-believe.

It's in this make-believe world where you can be whatever you want to be; *whatever you are prepared to work really hard at being* because this "make-believe world" may very well become your new reality – YOU MUST BELIEVE THIS OF YOURSELF AND FOR YOURSELF. So stop thinking as if you are "limited" to your own world and instead follow high in the footsteps of the world's most successful people.

Chapter 1 ~ Know Thyself

The power of 'Thought" is a real power. Consider this, thoughts can change your mood, make you cry or make you laugh. Thoughts can be read on camera. For example, just watch Jack Nicholson in "One Flew Over the Cuckoo's Nest." It's a scene where he first joins in the group of mental patents and he watches silently as they have a discussion. Watch how without saying a word, he can let you read his mind, so you know exactly what he's thinking at that moment. Thoughts, therefore, can travel from one mind through a TV screen or across a room to another mind. Thoughts can attract what you think about. Thoughts can betray you or give you away. Thoughts can raise your stress levels or calm you down. Thoughts can be good or bad or even evil. Thoughts can make you sick or can heal you. And let me finish this with a quote somewhat out of context, but it does apply *"Cogito, ergo sum,"* (Latin: *"I think, therefore I am"*) coined by the French philosopher René Descartes in his *Discourse on Method* (1637).

So, whether you believe in the power of visualization, or you think it's all "Mumbo Jumbo," it's up to you, but the art of visualization is a scientifically proven skill used by the worlds' most successful people.

By the way, a "skill" can be learned, and it's, in fact, a well-developed process or method of thinking specific images that stimulate the natural power of your mind to create this *vortex of success* spinning in your favor. This power is like a compass, except you control the direction the needlepoints in. Using the power of thought to create, direct and control images in your mind is a deliberate tool for inspiration and success and can improve your life.

The world's most successful people consistently use the *power of thought* as a tool to their advantage. They know that you attract what you think and you become what you think. They know that you must consistently put the time and effort, along with your persistence, faith, patience, and expectations into this mix and the results will start appearing over time.

Okay, so how does this all work?

Well, let's keep this simple. It's been scientifically proven that your subconscious mind cannot distinguish "real" from "imagined' and will react to "thoughts" that you think, and will also "believe to be real" any thoughts that you repeatedly think again and again over time.

What's So Special About You?

You must have heard the line, *"Tell a lie long enough and they will believe it,"* well, it's the same here. So for example, if you tell yourself enough times (with belief) that you can't do something, even if you can, then you won't. By the same token, if you tell yourself *you can do it* (with belief) often enough your brain will begin to believe it and you will feel that inner confidence and that is called self-empowerment.

This lady said it best: Mary Kay Ash, who never went to school and yet became one of the greatest female entrepreneurs in American history said: *"If you think you can, you can. And if you think you can't, you're right".*

Furthermore, if you think a sad thought, your brainwave activity shifts, meaning that the neurons will shift to create a pathway. This pathway is clusters of cells in your brain working together to create your memories or your learned behaviors that then trigger your body to act in a way *consistent with what you imagined.* This is how learning new habits works, and the more the pathway is used, the more the "habit" is embedded. The particular shift that you create with a "thought" or an "image" will then reverberate throughout your body, and perhaps you will begin to "feel" excited or inspired or perhaps you will feel depressed and confused. *You ultimately control the thoughts you allow to play out in your mind, so play nice and to your advantage.*

Now, gifted with this power, the world's most successful people will tell you that visualization has worked for them, and it can work for you. Having said that, you have got to really plan your work and then work your plan towards success. You would be making your moves using a multi-layered campaign of hard and smart work, being consistent, staying focused, disciplined, plus using meditation with visualization and using as many of the 77 qualities on a daily basis, giving it all you have, and making the whole visualization process a new habit. Think about it, success is based on successful habits, and failure is based on continued bad habits.

Now, believe it or not, but some people can't "visualize" an image in their mind's eye. It's like they are "mentally blind." This condition is called Aphantasia. Check out this new report by the BBC **Aphantasia: A life without mental images:** http://www.bbc.com/news/health-34039054

Chapter 1 ~ Know Thyself

Essentially, some people just can't imagine for example their dog or cat or their kid's face. No matter how hard they try to picture an image, they have no success. It's believed that this condition can be fixed because the mind is like a muscle and it needs to be worked correctly.

My suggestion is that if you have this condition, then it's time to take action if you already haven't. Try reading up on Aphantasia as well as some books on visualization, and learn memory courses because when using your memory, you develop focus and train your brain to get clarity in creating new images in your mind.

Finally, take a meditation course or use meditation with Yoga. I believe that to get any muscle working to an optimum you need to work out the best exercises and work them consistently.

Below I have an exercise for anyone who wants to improve their mental imagery as well as their concentration. I have used this exercise over the years in my courses and for myself.

Sit close enough to the candle, so you are comfortably able to "cup" your hands around the candle safely and feel the warmth of the flame.

Exercise #1   5-minute Candle and the Puppy Exercise

Now, I want you to know that the average person has around 70 thoughts per minute going on in their mind. That's 70 thoughts per minute! That's a lot of clutter. What we want to do is reduce that clutter down to *1 thought per minute*.

This exercise will sharpen your mind like never before. Your success relies on how well you can focus on the task at hand because your focus is the 'glue' that keeps all the building blocks of your dreams together. When you get distracted, it's like letting acid drip onto your focus. The acid eats into your focus, and the more distracted you get, the less your tasks, goals or dreams are fulfilled. So we are going to strengthen your focus and develop/sharpen your imagery.

Get yourself settled into a comfortable position with *no distractions*. Then light a candle, turn off all other lights and get comfortable about 2 feet in front of it.

What's So Special About You?

Take three deep relaxing breaths to start. Remember to breathe in through the nose and out through the mouth, and it is okay to make breath sounds if you want. Now, continue to breathe in and out like an ocean of relaxation. Find your natural breathing rhythm. Now as you do, I want you to observe the candle in peace and quiet; just you and the flame as one. Breathe, relax and still your mind by looking deep into the flame. Feel free to blink naturally as you will. Notice the colors of the flame: yellow, white, orange, bluish, purple and what other colors can you see? Don't stare at the flame, just look into it.

Each time you become aware that your "thoughts" have ventured off to something else, bring your mind back to the flame and remember to keep breathing. Look at the colors, the shapes, think on the flame. Your mind will wander off again and again and again, but just keep bringing it back to the flame. It's like a little puppy running off, and you simply pick the puppy up and bring it back. Please, be patient and gentle with yourself in this five-minute exercise. I promise you, it might appear to drive you crazy for the first five minutes, however, the more you practice this exercise of disciplining your mind and redirecting your thoughts, and reducing the amount of *thought-clutter*, the more you will open doors to tranquility. And in the energy of tranquility you will feel peace; a deeper peace from which new creative springs will pour forth to revitalize your body and your mind. Work on this exercise until you can get your mind to be still for a couple of minutes of stillness before moving onto the next exercise.

Exercise #2   Candle and Thought Visualization Exercise

Hopefully, you have practiced to still your mind before moving onto this exercise. Okay, this exercise will bring your imagery to life in your mind and sharpen your mental skills like never before.

Now before we begin, I would like you to get some coloring pencils and paper and then set them aside but close by. Then get settled into a comfortable position with *no distractions*. Then light a candle, turn off all other lights and get comfortable about 2 feet in front of it.

Take three deep relaxing breaths to start. Remember to breathe in through the nose and out through the mouth, and it is okay to make breath sounds if you want. Now continue to breathe in and out like an ocean of relaxation, and as you do I want you to observe the candle in

Chapter 1 ~ Know Thyself

peace and quiet; just you and the flame as one. Breathe, relax and still your mind by looking deep into the flame. Notice the colors of the flame: yellow, white, orange, bluish, purple and what other colors can you see? Don't stare at the flame, just look into it.

Just like the last exercise, each time you become aware that your thoughts have ventured off to somewhere else, bring your mind back to the flame and remember to keep breathing. Once you feel that your mind has settled and that you are in the peace of tranquility, then begin breathing a little deeper, almost like you are inhaling the soothing warmth of the candle flame. Then as you look into the flame, realize that this flame holds the mystery of the past itself; all the way back through the centuries to the very dawn of our human existence.

The deeper you look into the flame, the more seductive the flame becomes, ready to reveal its ancient past. And as you watch the flame I want you to *sense within yourself an emotion* that being in this moment means to you. Now I know you will feel relaxed, but I want you to sense deeper for another emotion that you are feeling at this moment. Don't force an emotion or a "thought," just breathe; relax and be in the moment with the flame and the stillness of your environment. Trust that the word to describe your deeper emotion will come to you in this silence. Be patient and be open to receiving. Meanwhile, if your thoughts wander off again, simply bring the little puppy back to this moment (free from reacting negatively.)

Once you feel that you have received the word that describes the deeper emotion you are feeling, other than "relaxed," then sit in that emotion for a time, still breathing in through the nose and out through the mouth.

Then when you feel ready, I want you to close your eyes and notice that the flame has left an "imprint" on your mind's eye. Also, notice that you can still see the "glow" of the flame through your eyelids.

Now, while still keeping your eyes closed, look at the imprinted flame image in your mind, then slowly and carefully lift your hands to both sides of the candle, almost like you are "cupping" your hands around the candle to where you can feel the flame's warmth on your hands.

What's So Special About You?

You should have your hands cupped around the candle flame, but because your eyes are closed, you will actually have your hands cupped around the mental image of the flame imprinted in your mind's eye. Your brain will know it's a real image because your brain senses the warmth from the flame on your hands and so to your brain the image is real. Still with your eyes closed and breathing as the ocean, "see" the image of your hands cupped around the imprinted flame.

This action keeps the reality of the image alive in your mind. You should still be able to see the flame's mental imprint, feel its warmth in your hands and see the glow behind your eyelids. All you need to do is relax, breathe and continue to "see" the image of the flame in your mind's eye as you saw it moments before and continue to 'feel' that other emotion. Live in this moment for a while and be patient, relaxed and breathe gently during this time. Please don't be thinking "time" per se, just feel when it's time to leave. Then gently open your eyes to see the flame and your hands cupped around it. Then move your hands to your cheeks and take in a fresh breath… exhale and enjoy this moment.

Finally, take your coloring pencils and begin to draw the flame you saw. Be very detailed and specific with what you recall in your mind and what you draw on the paper. Try drawing and coloring the flame with the same *deeper emotion* you had while being in tranquility with the flame. Connecting your image to that deeper emotion or your deeper emotion to that image reinforces in your mind that the image is "real." That's why your success imagery must have an emotion attached because it's the emotion – that *feeling* that brings to life the pictures in your mind and stimulates the vortex synergy of what it is you are trying to create. This action will further reinforce your mental and emotional recall ability, and your ability to communicate to your mind the types of thoughts and feelings you want to set your directional compass towards. This then *constitutes* the beginning of your success becoming real.

Do this exercise three times a week to expand your imagery muscle, your focus and your personal power. Ultimately, this exercise will prepare you for the most advanced work as you go along.

These exercises are the foundation that will help you strengthen your mind, break old habits and acquire new successful habits, improve your memory, live longer by reducing stress, open yourself up to your intuition, induce lucid dreams, reach your goals and achieve your dreams. It's worth doing these exercises as often as you can, even drawing and coloring the flames because each time is a new and empowering experience. *Remember your bigger picture and <u>why</u> you are investing your time and energy into these exercises.*

Keep your bigger picture in your mind and work your butt off to make your dreams happen.

For an empowering example meet, Sara Blakely; who is a big believer in using visualization to become successful. Sara recently gave a speech at the Woman's Leadership Exchange, where she explained that her goals were, *"To be self-employed, invent a product that she could sell to a lot of people, and to create a business that would be able to fund itself."* She then wrote her goals down, and she worked her butt off to make them her reality.

Sara, like the rest of the world's most successful people, know that the daily practice of visualizing and feeling that your dreams are already complete *(as if you are living in the vibration of that success)* can create that vortex spinning, attracting all that you need to support you in reaching your goals and your dreams *earlier*.

Having said that, realize that there are no guarantees of success but that at least now you are listening to the world's most successful people who advise you to be on this visualization path of success and happiness. Moreover, as I said earlier, this action then constitutes the beginning of your success becoming real.

Check out Sara Blakely – Tips for Success on YouTube.

MEANWHILE: BACK IN CLASS

Clearly, the students know that they have a massive mountain to climb and so far during this first week it looks like they are stepping up to the challenge. However, looks can be deceiving.

For example, one student quit over the first weekend. She told me that she just could not get comfortable with getting up in front of the class and doing the improvisation scenes. She said she felt the pressure of everyone watching her and she couldn't take it anymore. I tried to reassure her but to no avail. She had made up her mind to get out fast. She's only twenty-one years old, but I am sure it is a decision that will affect her for the rest of her life in many subtle ways.

Just think about it for a moment. Your life was never fully lived because at 21 you were too afraid to live it fully. All the places you missed, all the people you never met, all the opportunities that never happened, in fact, what could have been a full life lived will never be written and as such never experienced. I hope you are not like this.

Also, I already noticed in the first week that a few students had missed a day here or a day there. Perhaps they needed some private time to make quick mental adjustments – in other words, *"What the hell did I get myself into?"*

For those of you that are interested – It's time to get familiar and refer to your workbook. Please visit my site:

www.77GlobalVillage.com

Chapter 2 ~ Facing Inner Fear

FACING INNER FEAR
(Chapter 2 – Week 2)

"Real courage is being scared to death and saddling up anyway."

- John Wayne - Legendary Movie Star

The ability to adapt, to be flexible, will be your greatest asset throughout your lifetime. Change is inevitable and the world's most successful people embrace change.

Employers are looking for individuals who understand and demonstrate the flexibility and adaptability necessary to be successful in a dynamic environment.

"Fear" is an unclear and unpleasant emotion that is felt in anticipation of something, someone or even a situation that you perceive to be unpleasant. The fear can be real or imagined. The fear can cause a feeling of worry, nervousness, anxiety, and uneasiness, apprehension, or it can be extreme, like chronic stress, panic, feeling hopeless, overwhelmed, and even thinking or literally feeling that you need to fight for your life.

Psychiatry defines anxiety as a relatively permanent state of worry and nervousness occurring in a variety of mental disorders, usually accompanied by compulsive behavior or panic attacks. It is an abnormal sense of fear, nervousness, and apprehension about something that might happen in the future.

The truth is that your inner fears may look fearsome. They may even feel real, but they are NOT real. I know that you may be able to *understand that concept intellectually*; however, once you *emotionalize the concept* into your belief systems, the *illusion shatters*, and you will set yourself free. The truth is that the inner fears which you may allow to paralyze yourself from making decisions or from taking actions, or which *overwhelm* you and stop you from reaching your full potential - don't really exist. They are not real. You create it all. You conjure them up like magic.

You make the fear **FEARSOME!**

What's So Special About You?

The truth is that your inner fear is only **F**ake **E**vidence **A**ppearing **R**eal. It's an illusion. No matter how afraid you feel about getting up to try an exercise like improvising on the spot or public speaking, or wearing a clown's nose in public, or seeing yourself on camera, or letting go of negative habits, you are only going to feel the FEAR because that's what you have put in its place. You built the wall, and only you can bring the wall down with some help and guidance.

I always tell my students that FEAR is each person's opportunity to discover their courage, walk through the fire, and learn that each of them can and WILL survive.

You will survive, and then you will thrive!

MEANWHILE: BACK IN CLASS

The second week of the course was about getting the students to give up their perceived *control* of situations or things. Acting is about giving up control to the other person, but people want to feel safe, and to do that, they like to take control. So, I take the control away from the students and place them into a feeling of uncertainty, to see how well they adjust to change. Being uncertain can be an unsettling emotion, and we all strive to feel certain in life. The truth is, being uncertain can bring out the best in all of us.

The students had to learn to trust in their teacher, their instincts, and NOT their old habits, and they needed to go with the flow. It's the same in real life when you begin your first day on a new job, and you're trying to find your way of doing things.

It's not easy being in a new situation at first, but you push through the feelings of uncertainty, learn the ropes, and make little tweaks as you go. You wouldn't go into the boss's office on the first day to debate him on company procedures, because if you did, yes, you would be fired. The point I'm making is that you'd be trying to get the boss to "change" because you don't want to change.

Think of people you know, who like to have everything under their control. How about yourself? How do you try to control things or people or situations?

Chapter 2 ~ Facing Inner Fear

Most people from all walks of life prefer to be settlers rather than pioneers or adventurers. As an actor or a business leader or a person who wants success in their life, you MUST be fearless in your willingness to try new things and give up control.

In order to allow change, you must have a willingness to let go.

Let's see how you do with the next 8 of 77 empowering qualities that the world's most successful people use to create fabulous happiness and success. **Remember, the box on the left (#1) is empowering, and (#5) is self-defeating, and (#3) is halfway.**

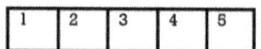

How do you rate with the best - ROUND 2

Successful people tend to be or have:

9/Courageous: They are courageous to try new things, face difficulties, uncertainty, or even a certain degree of pain without being overcome by fear or being derailed from a chosen course of action. They have the courage to stand up for themselves, for others and for what they believe in. [How courageous are you?]

10/Self-Confidence: They trust in their abilities to cope and succeed in situations; however, like anyone, their level of confidence will shift from high to low depending on the situation. For example, you may be a very confident and capable pilot; however, you may not feel so confident at first when learning to scuba dive. Remember, the world's most successful people are confident in their abilities to learn, make adjustments and thrive. [How confident are you in your abilities to learn and thrive?]

11/Build Relationships: They believe in making new relationships as well as in keeping the ones they have. However, they will break a poor relationship if they need to because they know that keeping great relationships is a big part of their success. [On what scale do you agree that keeping great relationships is a big part of your success?]

What's So Special About You?

☐☐☐☐☐ **12/Enthusiastic:** The world's most successful people know that nothing was ever achieved without enthusiasm. [How enthusiastic are you to take action when you get inspired?]

☐☐☐☐☐ **13/Decisive:** They show an ability to make decisions, quickly, firmly and clearly. [How decisive are you?]

☐☐☐☐☐ **14/Excellent Listeners:** They know to be silent and let others share their opinions. When they listen, they don't hold their breath waiting to find a spot to jump in with their thoughts. They are actually, mindful, attentive and present with the other person speaking because they truly want to understand. [How good of a listener are you?]

☐☐☐☐☐ **15/Sincere:** They care about people, humanity, business and they honor their word. They are honest people who show no pretense, no falsehoods, and no deception. How sincere are you and do you honor your word?]

☐☐☐☐☐ **16/Loyal:** Napoleon Bonaparte once said that *"The greatest gift one man can give another is loyalty."* They know that loyalty can be a double-edged sword. Loyalty <u>at all costs</u> is not their mantra, so don't break the law and ruin the loyalty bestowed. Loyalty is earned. They offer loyalty and will support you and fight for you, but do not break their trust. Loyalty works both ways and is considered "High value" in business and life. Don't blow it. [On what scale are you loyal?]

What's your score for round 2?

From the total of 8 questions, tally up and give yourself a 1, 2, 3, 4, or 5 for each tick you placed in the appropriate box as below.

1	2	3	4	5

Can you see where you are on par with them and where you need improvement? Okay so then pick one weakest to change and set a deadline for yourself. By the way, are you being consistent in dealing with the other weakness from the first chapter or did you forget?

FAKE EVIDENCE APPEARING REAL

One of the best ways to "let go," is to *practice* letting go. When we successfully break our emotional attachments to the "what is," that is holding us back, then we allow room for growth. However, letting go can also mean going into fear, and then people make so many excuses as to why they can't or won't let things go.

The truth is that fear is a by-product of the feeling of helplessness, and if you go deeper you will find the truth, and the truth in fear's case, is called *low self-esteem*. Remember, confidence and love are the foundation stones to success and happiness. However, most people allow FEAR to hold them back.

Some of the main inner fears people have are:

- Fear of failure
- Fear of being themselves
- Fear of reaching their true and full potential
- Fear of taking risks
- Fear of making mistakes
- Fear of rejection
- Fear of going beyond your comfort zone
- Fear of success

Remember what I told you about fear at the start of this chapter – it's **F**ake **E**vidence **A**ppearing **R**eal. It may feel real, but it's not, and unless you *are willing to experience the discomfort* of going through the FEAR, you will never change or progress in the direction you wish you would, or should, or MUST!

In fact, millions of gifted people are so consumed by their own perceived "fear" of rejection, failure, and negative self-talk, etc., that they may never learn the gifts of their true self, and the effects they can have on others and the world. All because of this FEAR, and the feeling of helplessness. This is tragic.

What's So Special About You?

Let's turn tragedy into victory by looking at inner FEAR FACTORS. First; you are not born with fear, it is a learned habit, and therefore it can be unlearned. I want you to read below to see if you can identify with any of these main fears.

- Fear of public speaking: "Oh my God NO! Anything but that!" The idea of getting up in front of people staring at you, waiting for you to speak, makes you almost want to faint. You feel you just can't do it.
- Fear of failure: You just have to be perfect at what you are doing or else you feel a failure. For you, failure is unthinkable.
- Fear of taking risks: Always ready to play safe, unwilling to try something new. You just can't stand change.
- Fear of making mistakes: "I am imperfect, flawed, and weak."
- Fear of rejection: "People will not accept me for who I am. They will never like me."
- Fear of being judged: "People will make fun, call me a freak, and talk about me behind my back".
- Fear of going beyond your comfort zone: "I will look like a fool. I just can't do that. It's too hard. I'm not good enough. It seems like so much work. I'm too afraid to try".
- Fear of not looking good: "I need my hair and nails just right. My makeup needs to be perfect. I must have just the right clothes on".
- Fear of making decisions: "What if I am wrong?"
- Fear of being inadequate: "I just can't be like them. I'm not good enough".
- Fear of being unmasked and being seen as a fake: "They will see I'm not like that. They will see that I am a faker".
- Fear of being "labeled": "I can't stand being labeled as this or that, or being put in a box. They want to limit me, control me, and stop me from being myself".
- Hopelessness: This is a feeling of not knowing what to do or how to do it. (Hopelessness) usually, leads to depression.

Chapter 2 ~ Facing Inner Fear

- Depression: Millions of people feel like they just can't get out of bed or step out the front door. Life seems overwhelming and can include loss of appetite or overeating, problems concentrating or making decisions, and people may even contemplate suicide. Some do take the tragic step of suicide.
- Self-loathing: People often feel they're not good enough for anything and dwell on their own shortcomings, including exaggerating them out of all proportion just so they end up feeling even worse about themselves. Self-loathing is a hatred of yourself or your actions. "I deserve this; it must be my fault."
- Fear of success: It may sound silly but with success comes more responsibility and more demands on you, more deadlines, the more potential pressure to keep the success going. Your anxiety levels go through the roof because what if you can't take it anymore? Therefore, it's easier to look successful and only do what's needed to keep you up and running, but you never really push beyond your set limits to become truly successful.

If you can identify with any of the above, then perhaps, you are experiencing one fear or another. Successful people don't do "FEAR"; they eat it for breakfast and then have a successful "fart" afterward.

What you need to do is learn to develop some fear-slaying strategies.

For starters, remember that FEAR is a choice. FEAR does not mean DANGER. It's different. Danger can be real, but fear is a choice. You choose to feel fear and build it into – a paralyzing condition that you feel you cannot get through.

When you hear that little voice whisper the words in your head, that *"You can't do that"* or *"You're not good enough"* or *"You're not special enough"* or just simply, *"Give it up,"* remember, it's not true! Don't give in to that negative inner voice of FEAR. What is true is that YOU DECIDE if you can do something or if you can't do it. That decision should be based on you being honest and truthful with yourself.

What's So Special About You?

Know the difference between "I can't do that" and "*I can't do that.*" There are universal laws in this life worth having a healthy respect for or fear of crocodiles, a crazy guy with a handgun, or even standing in front of a fast-moving truck and saying *"It will only pass through me,"* because it won't, it will smash you to bits. So please be responsible and know the difference between real danger-producing fear and your inner perceived fear.

Your fear may truthfully be that you *don't* have all the information, or technical information or the next steps to achieve what you need to achieve, and you really can't do it. But that's not perceived fear, that's a lack of all the information needed to make a move. Don't use the "lack of" to stop you from taking actions like brainstorming solution-based ideas, or doing the research needed to help build your confidence, so you can get clarity and begin taking the actions needed to move forward again.

Something may be required of you that you genuinely can't do and that's okay. Just be responsible, know thyself, and ask yourself, *"Am I saying I <u>can't do it</u> out of inner fear?"* and if the answer is yes, then perhaps you should just do it and break through that fear.

Chapter 2 ~ Facing Inner Fear

The hard truth is that if you really want what you claim you want, then you will find a way. You will go to the four corners of the earth. You will stay up all night. You will work three jobs. You will survive war, abuse, poverty. You will do it. How do I know? Because the world's most successful people have had to face those same hard truths themselves, and they did the "impossible." They did it before you, and other successful people will do it after you. If you really want it, then you will do it. Trust that hard truth. Own it and do it.

Usually, you will find that your perceived fear is an inner struggle between your fear of failure and your fear of success. You see, fear of failure will paralyze you into not taking the action needed to overcome its hold on you. For example, the fear of being publicly humiliated will stop people in their tracks from taking action.

And here is the kicker: Usually, people aren't even aware of the perceived struggle between the fears going on inside them. This inner turbulence goes on "under the radar." People will avoid thinking about it or even talking about it because to do so brings their awareness of the struggle within them and their weaknesses; that if they only had the courage to deal with them; life would change forever. They turn to distractions like television, video games, etc. for their great night of inspiration.

Here is some wonderful advice: don't project your perceived "fears" into the future because you are taking away all hope. When we lose hope, we die inside. Do not take away your future hope and leave your future self with the feeling of being hopeless and abandoned. You must look at the positive aspects of life and take positive actions, and the future <u>will</u> change for the brighter. You are not your past failings. This is a new day.

Remember, "What you think, you become," so think positive and *take empowering actions.*

FOR MORE IN-DEPTH STUDY OF THIS CHAPTER, PLEASE VISIT www.77GlobalVillage.com

What's So Special About You?

LETTING GO
(Chapter 3 – Week 3)

"Learn to burn your old bridges of habit and leave yourself no escape route except to go forward."

Christopher Healy – Coach, presenter, author.

The 21st century marketplace demands that people have a broad range of skills and experiences and not just training in one skill. Learning more skills places you at an advantage, ahead of the pack. This means learning to let go and move on to new uncertain terrain; learning yet again, always adding what you have learned to your list of growing assets.

This chapter is about letting go of the old and starting new. It takes courage and strength of character to make the commitment to burn your old bridges of habit and move forward into new uncertain terrain. That's exactly what is needed if you want to be on a path to success. This third week was also a continued challenge for the students as each week they had to stay focused and challenge their old habits with new habits. Letting go of old habits can be very stressful, and that _reality_ made some students quit.

Do you consider yourself to be a quitter?

How about in your own (positive or negative) self-talk?

Do you keep a strong face but inside you're just holding on by your fingernails?

Do you personally know of anyone who is a real "control freak?"

How about you?

Chapter 3 ~ Letting Go

MEANWHILE: BACK IN CLASS

After the first two weeks of introducing "change" to the students, the third week was about bonding them together as a team. This week saw the students having to step up to the reality of having a twenty-page scene from the movie *"The Breakfast Club"* completely memorized, ready to go. Unfortunately, most students weren't ready at all.

The students were now faced with their *"procrastination"* head-on, as in a train wreck!

They also did an "Italian" exercise; by saying twenty pages of text as fast as they could without thinking of the words, which was pressure enough. Each time a team member made a mistake or paused meant that everyone started again from the beginning. It was like the students were on a twenty-mile hike, and each of them was responsible for each other.

You can't get past the finish line if your partner can't get past it with you. This exercise forced the students to drop their "dramas" and work through their individual "stuff." They had to learn to co-operate and build the "team" dynamic, or they would fall into frustration and blame each other until something cracked, resulting in a walkout. It's called **TEAM** dynamic: ***Together Each Achieves More.***

In the business world, this "in the trenches chaos" is unacceptable and show business *is* the business world. This means that people need to learn to work together by listening, respecting others' views, and giving up the "ego control" of trying to dominate the situation. This exercise is a perfect example because instead of complaining about the other teammate, they need to try helping the other teammate to get their part done, so everybody wins!

Successful people know how to listen and inspire their team to create results together, no matter how bad the problems seem to be.

At the end of the day, people have to let go of what's holding them back or let go of what's blocking the team dynamic and learn to work together to achieve more together. It's called *win win.*

What's So Special About You?

Now, for your study, let's see how well you answer the next round of winning qualities.

HOW DO YOU RATE WITH THE BEST – ROUND 3

Below are the next 7 of 77 empowering qualities that the world's most successful people use to create fabulous happiness and success. How do you rate? **Remember, the box on the left (#1) is empowering, and (#5) is self-defeating, and (#3) is halfway.**

1	2	3	4	5

Successful people tend to be or have:

17/Committed: They will give their "all" towards a focal point and make positive changes towards success, regardless of the personal discomfort they may endure. [On what scale do you give your "all" in tasks that must be done, and not necessarily because you love doing them?]

18/Protect Their Downside: They take the time to learn the downside of a project or a company before jumping in. They know the value of recognizing their downside as well as knowing when to get out. [How well do you protect your downside in doing something where even risk is risky?]

19/Independent: They cherish their independence. They are free-spirited thinkers who do not require validation from others. They can work independently, meaning they take the lead, do the research, struggle through and get the work done. [How independent are you?]

20/Create Great Experiences: They know how to create "great personal experiences" for their customers and not just sell them products. Look at some of the big brands like Microsoft, Apple, Facebook, Starbucks, and Amazon, just to name a few. They offer their customers experiences that are exciting, inspiring and that people can

Chapter 3 ~ Letting Go

get emotional about. [In your business or line of work, how much do you offer "great personal experiences" to your clients or customers?]

21/Meet Deadlines: They plan, set and work toward realistic deadlines; for they understand that deadlines are the clear benchmarks of accomplishment in the real world and are absolutely critical to success. [How well do you achieve your deadlines?]

22/Delegate: They are masters at delegation. They allocate wisely the right tasks to the right people. They know that to delegate successfully is to provide direction and an opportunity for the team to get hands-on experience, take ownership and lead the way. [How well do you delegate?]

23/Differentiate: *To perceive the difference between things; to discriminate.* They have a keen eye for winners and losers, gold or fool's gold. They are masters at distinguishing or separating themselves from their competitors. [Do you have a keen eye for the unique and different, or should I say between gold and fool's gold?]

What's your score for round 3?

From the total of 7 questions, tally up and give yourself a 1, 2, 3, 4, or 5 for each tick you placed in the appropriate box as below.

1	2	3	4	5

Can you see where you are on par with them and where you need improvement? Are you too set in your ways to make improvements or are you willing to create yourself anew? Are you being *consistent* with the other weaknesses from previous chapters?

LET'S DEAL WITH LETTING GO

First up, understand that "letting go" is liberating because, in truth, you are liberating yourself from the chains of negativity, your past failures, trying to control things or people, and by "letting go" you place yourself on the path to happiness and freedom. Letting go can be very uncomfortable, and this is the main reason people won't allow themselves to improve their lives because the "change" means feeling uncomfortable, stressful or fearful.

The world's most successful people throw themselves into "uncomfortable" all the time, and make the changes needed to be on the top of their game.

Today, I would like you to practice letting go, and this begins with you being willing to give up your sense of "control." People try to control many things in their lives because they are pushing their own agenda. For example, we try to control other people, and this can be seriously FRUSTRATING!

Here is a big tip for the wise, learn to control what you can control and accept this liberating truth; you cannot control other people's actions; what they say, or what they do, or how they think...so let it go. However, you can control how you think, feel and react.

Some of the "letting go" may include letting go of your old negative beliefs, your inner fears, any resentment you may be holding against others, any guilt you carry, and learning to forgive yourself and others. Many people allow internal negative thinking to destroy their lives. It is that little voice (again) in your head that says "you can't do it" or "shut up you're not good enough." Most people believe the "internal lies" they tell themselves on a daily basis, and never break free of their slavery of feeling mediocre.

To free yourself and be one of the world's most successful people, you need to replace those negative thoughts with more empowering thoughts. So for example, "I will never reach my dream," to be replaced by "I will achieve my dream by taking at least one action towards my dream each day."

Then actually perform that action. Take any action as small as it may be to move you forward on the path of success. Just by doing this action, you are destroying the negative thought and replacing it with your positive action.

Another example, "I just don't have the confidence to do this," and the replacement could be, "Everyone starts at the beginning, and if I continue, I will gain the confidence."

Watch for some of the telltale signs of negative thinking (and solutions) like:

- Using your emotions as clear evidence about something and not looking at the facts. "I just know it" type of thinking could be coming from a negative feeling. Make sure you look at the facts before making a decision.

- Watch for "All or nothing" type of thinking, for example, "All television shows are mindless" or "Used car salesmen are crooks." Remember life is many shades and not just black and white.

- Watch for negating your own achievements by saying "Oh I was just lucky', or "I can't believe I just did that" or "I did it because I wore my "'lucky" sweater."

- Don't exaggerate what might be just an awkward situation into a big, awful, horrible situation. Just see it for what it is, no more and no less.

- Watch for rehashing negative situations. Actually, my wife called me out on this last night, over a situation that I kept bringing up from time to time over a few hours. Rehashing negative crap over and over again is really inviting negative energy to affect your body, your mind and not allowing yourself to get your spirits up because you keep inviting the negativity in again to bring your energy down into anxiety, worry, feeling lousy or in a slump.

- Be careful of all the "Yeah-buts" you use in your day; like "Yeah but" I can't do that or "Yeah-but" who would ever want me?" Also, become aware of how many times you say, "I should," because this most likely means that you will not. In my acting classes, I teach that "acting" is about being specific with the details of character and the situations, and not using generalities. Therefore, the words "I should" are too general and offer no real commitment. Try saying "I will."

- Try not to jump to conclusions like; "Something must be wrong if it's taking this long" or "If they liked me why didn't they turn up?"

- Don't just focus on the problem, focus on the possible solutions.

- Watch for all - and I do mean ALL the excuses and the blame, blame, blame you are thinking and verbalizing. Stop playing the role of 'victim,' instead, take ownership of the disaster, focus on the possible solutions and lead yourself forward like a true Hero. Breathe in inspiration and be at peace within.

- Watch for comparing yourself with others. Comparing yourself can be a slippery slope even to "gain perspective," because "comparing" means either *less than* or *better than the* type of thinking. Instead, I would suggest that you must look to others to be inspired and learn from them.

- Watch how many times you may be saying "Sorry," for example, "Sorry for interrupting, but can you pass the salt?" Just ask nicely "Excuse me, can you pass the salt, please'. Just be aware of when a "sorry" really applies.

- Be aware of how you may be thinking "Small." How would it be to think "BIG" for a change?

- Don't be living on auto-pilot with all the same old negative beliefs. Become more in the present and in the moment.

Chapter 3 ~ Letting Go

> Remember, you are not your past, and so you can allow yourself to let your past go, allow the new principle that you are practicing to formulate within you and change becomes real. You are setting yourself on a path to a new future.

Now, to be clear here, I understand that some circumstances may not be your fault, but how you react to them and let it control your emotional state, your thinking and your actions are your choices. Be aware of it and take ownership. Once you become aware of negative thinking, you can change it for the better.

First, become aware of how you think and speak negatively, and then verbalize a more empowering thought. By applying this simple tactic, you will change that feeling of negativity into a feeling of empowerment.

I am not suggesting that you suppress what you are feeling or that you avoid it. I am not suggesting that you avoid confrontation. I am suggesting that you be aware of what you are feeling, recognize why are you feeling this emotion and not to use the 'blame' routine. Learn to express when and where appropriate and then release yourself of the feeling by breathing and not rehashing it again and LET IT GO.

Also, when you are expressing yourself, watch for how you use your tone of voice. Do you speak in a condescending way to the person or do you get your point across while still being respectful? Think about how you would like to be approached and spoken to. Try to find the "win-win" for both of you. Here is an idea, if time permits ask yourself in advance of the possible confrontation – ask, "How could I handle that better?", and then go in with the right intentions.

Try practicing compassion, tolerance, and kindness; this will convert any negative emotion into a more empowering emotion.

Remember, negative thoughts have an unhelpful and pessimistic effect on you, while positive and encouraging thoughts have an empowering effect on you – in every way – body, mind, and spirit, including how you interact with others. So be vigilant because to let go of these ways requires a serious and purposeful commitment from you.

MEANWHILE: BACK IN CLASS AGAIN

The students went *through* a roller coaster this week. They were set in their ways, unprepared, full of procrastination, distractions, overcoming negative self-talk, but they didn't quit. They actually discovered possibilities, the importance of focus, and started to believe that they could create themselves anew.

Normally, people don't think along these terms as *creating themselves anew* or *reinventing themselves*. Instead, people are running on autopilot, totally unaware of what's happening within them and around them. Just put in the hours, race home, eat and vegetate in front of the TV or online and then sleep it all off until the morning when it happens all over again.

If you the reader are taking all this information in, then you are or should be, thinking along these same terms in your efforts to renovate yourself like never before. Hopefully, you are questioning your own thoughts and beliefs.

Negative thinking is a real killer of hope and *successful people don't allow negative thinking into their lives because they know its destructive power. It's like sipping poison over a period of time.*

**FOR MORE IN-DEPTH STUDY OF THIS CHAPTER,
PLEASE VISIT** www.77GlobalVillage.com

PROCRASTINATION
(Chapter 4 – Week 4)

"You cannot escape the responsibility of tomorrow by evading it today."

~ Abraham Lincoln

 *Most people fail to achieve their dreams because they don't believe they can actually attain them. They get up each day on autopilot with no life goals in mind, no organized plan, and no thought on how to execute their dreams into reality; and if they might initially attempt any of the above, they procrastinate it all away.*

Procrastination is the number one killer of success, and it is reported that 85% of all people on planet earth procrastinate. That's 85% of the world's population!!

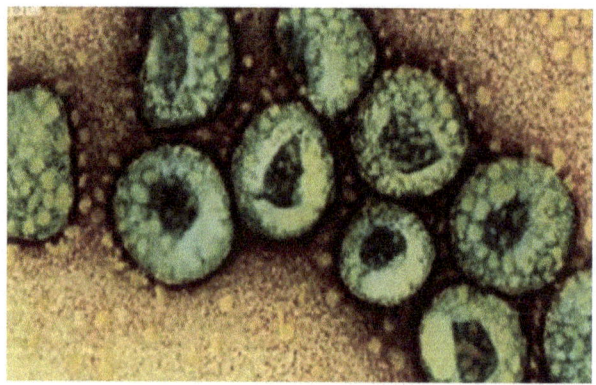

Look at it this way, if procrastination were a deadly virus, that would mean almost 6 billion people would be dead, and just over 1 billion would survive. Scary thought.

What does procrastination mean to you? In this chapter, we will look at procrastination, crack it open and go deep.

What's So Special About You?

MEANWHILE: BACK IN CLASS

This week we shot the twenty-page scene from the movie *"The Breakfast Club,"* and the procrastinators of the group had to do some serious cramming of their lines to be ready.

Interestingly enough, it was in this fourth week that we were beginning to witness some interesting results between what the students *said they would do* versus *what they actually did do*. Since the beginning of this course from Day 1, the students would say one thing, think another, and their actions told a different story yet. For example, the students agreed on day one that they would all arrive on time with me in the mornings, and have their work ready to go for that day. Well, it was as early as the second week that I could already see cracks in their work ethic. Many of them were walking in late, some had not memorized their lines, and yet they still thought that they were living up to their dreams.

I do believe it was Anthony Robbins who said, *"Dreams without actions are delusions."*

For the first three weeks, their words *(for the most part)* did not live up to their actions. In fact, if I was to put aside what they said about wanting to be successful, and focused my attention only on their physical actions, then a different story emerged.

Their actions of turning up late, missing days, excuses, blame, laziness, procrastination, tummy troubles, creating distractions and not having the work ready, revealed their inner more powerful belief: *"I can't live up to my dreams. I can't do this, but I'll pretend it."*

However, this fourth week began to show a turnaround. For example, the student's own words of being *committed and working hard* actually began to reflect their actions. Let us be truthful here; your words and actions must be in alignment, otherwise, you are deluding yourself.

So for the students, this means that now, for the most part, they are actually beginning to live up to wanting to live their dreams. Thoughts into actions mean they are beginning to BELIEVE. This then is their turning point!

Chapter 4 ~ Procrastination

Once they begin to believe what they are experiencing, their learning will be more potent, rapid and life-changing. However…

I'm DONE!
…Me Too!

Transformation always has casualties along the way, because, over the next few weeks, two more quit, and the remaining students had to drop the "pretense" and really pull themselves back 'in-line," to live up to the reality of what this course imposes on them. This "horrible" on-going reality demands that ALL students arrive on time, ready to work, no exceptions, *(unless they can show a doctor's note that they are sick)* otherwise no excuses, and no procrastination will be accepted. Each student made a commitment to live their dreams for the duration of the course. No commitment to hard work equals no dreams realized. Quitting is always an option, but so too is going the distance to success!

Of course, the unseen outcome behind all of these past weeks of coaching, discovery and working together has been developing the student's sense of *"self-discipline."*

For you the reader, you have had to consistently continue the discipline of reading this book alongside the other disciplines you already use in your daily life. Without developing a strong discipline to keep yourself in line and make progress, you are destined to fail. To be among the world's most successful people, you must *forge within yourself a strong self-discipline.*

For the students, these past four weeks have been about developing that discipline. For you, let's see how you do with the next round of empowering qualities that the world's most successful people use to create fabulous happiness and success.

What's So Special About You?

HOW DO YOU RATE WITH THE BEST – ROUND 4

Below are the next 8 of 77 empowering qualities that the world's most successful people use to create fabulous happiness and success. How do you rate? **Remember, the box on the left (#1) is empowering, and (#5) is self-defeating, and (#3) is halfway.**

| 1 | 2 | 3 | 4 | 5 |

Successful people tend to be or have:

24/ Prepared: They get what they need ready in advance (no procrastination) for a better, more amplified performance in all that they do. Remember my belief – *Proper Planning Prevents Poor Performance*. It's true. [How well do you prepare in advance?]

25/ Self Starter: These people are motivated, self-starters. They have a strong propose that gets them out of bed and propels them forward, combined with a magnetic reward that draws them through their days. [How much of a self-starter are you?]

26/ Organized: They are organized and are able to work in a systematic and efficient way. [Are you organized, able to work in a systematic and efficient way?]

27/ Excellent Manager: They know how to manage situations, people, their time, their health, their habits, their resources and their assets. [How good of a manager are you?]

28/ Know When To Say "No": That's right! The world's most successful people know when to say "No" to people, to an idea or a proposal. It's important to know how to tell brilliant ideas from brilliant distractions and then have the good sense to say "No" when needed. Are you the type that says "Yes" to everyone so often that you are run ragged doing everything for others and not enough for yourself? [How good are you are saying "No"?]

Chapter 4 ~ Procrastination

29/Self-disciplined: They know that self-discipline is the backbone of their success and they have the ability to control their impulses. [On what scale are you self-disciplined?]

30/Productive: They don't waste time, they use every minute when working hard to produce what they need. FYI - Successful people are productive between 50 - 60 plus hours a week. However, remember this; when being productive, they work hard at working **smart.** [When working, how truly productive are you?]

31/ Authentic: They live their "true self" in public. Being yourself is fulfilling, but it takes guts to walk through the land of conformity and still stand in the power of your true self. Know who you are. Know what you represent. And have the courage to be who you are. YOU are unique! [How authentic are you?]

What's your score for round 4?

From the total of 8 questions, tally up and give yourself a 1, 2, 3, 4, or 5 for each tick you placed in the appropriate box as below.

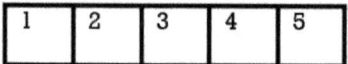

Can you see where you are on par with the world's most successful people? Where do you need improvement?

What's So Special About You?

PROCRASTINATION

To begin with, procrastination is a learned habit. You are not born with it, you learn it, and therefore you can unlearn it. Procrastination is the act of replacing high-priority actions or tasks with low-priority actions and thus putting off important tasks to a later time.

Psychologists suggest that procrastination can help some people deal with the anxiety connected with starting or completing any task or making a decision. Psychologists Schraw, Pinard, Wadkins, and Olafson have proposed that there are three criteria for a behavior to be classified as procrastination: it must be counterproductive, needless, and delaying. Psychological research also directly links procrastination to stress, a sense of guilt, crisis, loss of personal/professional productivity, and social disapproval for not meeting responsibilities or commitments.

These feelings when combined may promote further procrastination. While it is regarded as "normal" for people to procrastinate to some degree, it becomes a problem when it impedes normal functioning. Chronic procrastination may be a sign of an underlying psychological disorder. Even businesses are becoming increasingly aware of the productivity costs of procrastination and procrastinators usually, have lower grades and higher levels of stress and illness. Below I have added a link to an interesting video about what procrastination is. It's something to consider. Please check it out.

Watch this video on Vimeo: http://vimeo.com/9553205

HOW TO IDENTIFY IF YOU ARE A PROCRASTINATOR

I remember reading years ago, that 96% of people who attend the famous "Guru' workshops from around the world don't even act on the information they have paid hundreds of dollars to get. That means that only 4% take the actions needed while the other 96% are emotionally charged for a few days and within a few weeks are back to where they started off. This "inaction" makes them feel a little bit weaker, and so they buy another book or DVD or take another workshop, only to end up with the same result – feeling a little bit more negative about themselves for not taking the actions needed thereby to the massive negative weight already weighing them down.

Chapter 4 ~ Procrastination

So, according to those statistics, 96% of the people reading this book will do nothing with the life-changing information within; however 4% percent will take the steps suggested in this book, and by doing so, will change their life towards being more successful, happier and more rewarding.

Most people delay on taking the actions needed to get themselves moving in a positive direction, and others just over-analyze themselves into paralysis. They just keep running it over and over again in their minds but fail to take action. Apparently, there is 23% percent of people who suffer from chronic procrastinating, while another 50% can function but they still struggle with it. About 80%–95% of students also struggle with procrastination, leaving their work until the night before and then "cramming-it." *Talk about self-induced stress!!*

Procrastinators don't like deadlines and seek distractions to put doing tasks off until they go gangbusters, then try to get it all done in a few hours. Of course, their stress levels go through the roof, but procrastinators will sometimes try to defend what they "do" or don't do, by saying, they *"Perform better under pressure."* The truth, however, is that this is just their way of justifying why they keep avoiding getting things done. And as long as they continue to believe this "lie" they tell themselves, it's going to be very hard to get them to make any real change. It's not that they are "lazy," because there are many factors in explaining procrastination.

The psychological causes of procrastination appear connected with anxiety, a low sense of self-worth, as well as a self-defeating mentality, and of course, fear of failure.

For some individuals, procrastination may be symptomatic of a psychological disorder such as depression or ADHD, which is a problem causing inattentiveness, over-activity, impulsivity, or a combination of the above. People who suffer from chronic procrastination should seek professional help. There is no stigma attached, and your consultations are strictly confidential, so please make that move and get some help.

What's So Special About You?

Procrastination includes using the following:

- Procrastinators actively seek distractions like email, video games or television or are constantly going to social media sites to prevent themselves from doing the activity needing to be done
- Sometimes procrastinators blame external forces beyond their control
- Procrastinators will try to convince others that their behavior is not procrastinating, but rather delaying because a more important task is needed to be done, thereby avoiding the real task
- Procrastinators will overestimate or underestimate the time they have to get tasks done
- Procrastinators will avoid the situation, the task and even the location just to get out of doing the task. If that means avoiding school, then they will do so
- Procrastinators consistently make excuses and build up reasons in their heads as to why they can't get around to the task anytime soon
- Procrastinators actually believe that succeeding at a task requires that they "feel" like doing it and that working when "not in the mood" is counterproductive and below their high standard. Of course, it's just an embedded excuse that they hold true to their hearts

The truth is that procrastination is a cover-up leading to a deeper truth called FEAR OF FAILURE, which once again takes you back to *"What are you afraid of?"* Give that some more thought.

FOR MORE IN-DEPTH STUDY OF THIS CHAPTER, PLEASE VISIT www.77GlobalVillage.com

Chapter 5 ~ Breaking The Habit

BREAKING THE HABIT
(Chapter 5 - Week 5)

"The greatest discovery of my generation is that a human being can alter his life by altering his attitudes of mind."

William James US philosopher & psychologist
(1842 - 1910)

WHO AM I?

I am your constant companion. *I am* your greatest helper or heaviest burden. *I will* push you onward or drag you down to failure. *I am* completely at your command. *I am* managed with care -- you must be firm with me. Show me exactly how you want something done, and after enough lessons, I will do it automatically. *I am* the servant of all great people and, alas, of all failures. Those who are great, I have made great. Those who are failures, I have made failures. *I am* not a machine, though I work with the precision of a machine and the intelligence of a person. You may run me for profit or run me for ruin -- it makes no difference to me! Take me, train me, and be firm with me, and I will place the world at your feet. Be easy with me and I will destroy you ... Who Am I?

I AM HABIT

This fifth week the student's moral was scattered, their focus faded out, their energy depleted. This week they learned that being *"consistently"* on top of things was going to be a tough battle within one's self. In "story" terms, it's like a battle of Good versus Evil, but this time the stories are real. The inner conflicts are real. They reflect the internal struggle being played out by people everywhere, every minute of every day, even within yourself.

In the student's case, it's about experiencing a metamorphosis from their old ways of living life into a whole new empowering way of living life. It's not easy, but it's what you must awaken into if you want to live your dreams for real.

What's So Special About You?

The most successful of them will rise to the top of the mountain, while the rest are left behind in the mire of conflicting emotions, feeling like they will never have happiness or success. They just surrender to a belief that they have nothing special to offer.

For those of you who have gone through this book thus far and have done the exercises from the workbook, then you too have felt the inner battle of staying focused and motivated. You must realize that you need to keep going forward.

~ *"Don't give up on yourself, because you are worth the effort!"*

The world's most successful people know what's it like to feel alone, but they NEVER abandoned their beliefs and dreams. They NEVER accepted that they were second rate. They know that they had more to give and they always stayed true to that belief. So stay true to YOURS! *You are worth the effort!*

On the following page are the next 7 of 77 empowering qualities that the world's most successful people use to create fabulous happiness and success. Let's see how you rate. **Remember, the box on the left (#1) is empowering, and (#5) is self-defeating, and (#3) is halfway.**

1	2	3	4	5

Chapter 5 ~ Breaking The Habit

How do you rate with the best – ROUND 5

Successful people tend to be or have:

|☐|☐|☐|☐|☐| **32/Compassionate:** They share genuine concern and compassion for the misfortunes of others. They will often give money and <u>provide solutions</u> to ease suffering or to support the disadvantaged. [How compassionate are you?]

|☐|☐|☐|☐|☐| **33/Detail-Oriented:** They have the ability to get in there and see the details of a project or situation clearly. [On what scale are you the flexible type?

|☐|☐|☐|☐|☐| **34/Leaders:** They have the ability to empower, guide, direct or influence people. [On what scale are you a leader?]

|☐|☐|☐|☐|☐| **35/Fair:** They are able to take into account all sides based on their merits, without prejudice or favoritism. [How fair are you?]

|☐|☐|☐|☐|☐| **36/Proactive:** They make "change" happen. They use reasoning, planning, creativity and problem-solving skills to navigate the way ahead. They anticipate possible challenges, take the initiative, act in advance of a situation, rather than reacting to it. They think through logically and understand options clearly, weigh alternatives and make decisions to achieve their goals. [On what scale are you the proactive type?]

|☐|☐|☐|☐|☐| **37/They Sell Dreams:** They know how to package and sell dreams and not just products. They know that people everywhere have dreams and aspirations and they sell their products, concepts, and strategies to help people build and achieve their dreams. [How well do you sell dreams?]

What's So Special About You?

38/Resilient: For the most part, they have learned to adapt to and cope with stressful situations and then begin making progress again. It's not that they are invulnerable to stress, they have learned to cope. [How resilient are you?]

What's your score for round 5?

From the total of 7 questions, tally up and give yourself a 1, 2, 3, 4, or 5 for each tick you placed in the appropriate box as below.

1	2	3	4	5

Can you see where you are on par with the world's most successful people? Where do you need improvement?

MEANWHILE: BACK IN CLASS

I started the week by letting the students know that their first experience of going into the meat grinder known as the "Gladiatorial Games' was about to occur in the form of a mock TV commercial audition. I wanted them to see how they would react in stressful auditions and become aware of how stress and self-negativity destroy their performance, as opposed to when they are feeling relaxed, prepared and positive about themselves.

Remember, successful people don't go into panic mode when stress hits, they react calmly and work their way through it.

In truth, the students will subject themselves to so much more stress on themselves in the real audition. It's the same in the real world when people add extra stress stepping into that "all important career interview" only to let the stress ruin it completely. Or when people have to get up and speak in public!

When the students tried doing the TV commercial in four takes, many were not very well prepared, and as such, they felt failure once again. This tactic of getting it right in four takes impressed upon them the *critical importance of being fully prepared.* Imagine if you have a once-in-a-lifetime meeting with one of the world's most successful people.

Chapter 5 ~ Breaking The Habit

You are going to present to them one of your ideas, and you are putting yourself on the line to make a first impression. *Well, you had better be prepared.* Also, the students suffering from procrastination were going through some serious withdrawals. They had to keep on top of all the work of learning new lines and the accompanying physical movements in their current scenes, as well as do their character homework in the evening, and begin analyzing and memorizing their next work. *Remember, successful people have to know how to juggle multiple tasks with multiple people from minute to minute each day, and do it all with success in mind and not surrender.*

I Quit!

This was also the week another student quit the course because he had written out the wrong homework on a spare page that was useless. So, I simply took the page and gently tore it up, much to the shock and horror of the student in question.

I told him to throw this work in the bin and start again. Well, that was the last straw! He used the paper being torn up as an excuse to quit and not return. Even after I offered an apology with a simple explanation; that the work he handed in was useless and he needed to learn to let go of "useless" and move on, in other words, *adapt!*

The truth is when "shit happens" and it throws you off your game, (and it does happen quite often) he or she must learn NOT to take it personally but rather, work with the changes and then get on with it.

It's just like the world's most successful people. They won't allow themselves to get derailed because of "things that just happen." However, if they did get derailed, they took it in their stride and moved forward inspiring their team to do the same.

In order to change for the better, you need to let go of the "HABITS" and "BELIEFS" that hold you back. This week of stress for the students brought to the forefront their own negative beliefs and limiting habits. The students were now going into their innermost cave to see their personal enemy within, known as the Negative Ego.

What's So Special About You?

Your negative Ego is the voice in your head that says *"You can't do it."* Don't believe the internal lies. Your negative ego may be out of control if earlier in your life you decided not to take responsibility for many of your decisions. Instead, you may have allowed your negative ego to make all the "feel good, easy" choices for you, and you went along with it. But now you are attempting to take back control from your negative ego.

The problem is that your negative ego has been in power for so long, now it will play every dirty mind trick in the book to get you to stop making a positive change within yourself. Your negative ego likes the power you gave it, and it wants to keep the power.

By contrast, the world's most successful people have allowed positive habits to build their success instead of allowing negative habits to take over. Big difference!

IT'S TIME TO FACE IT.

It's time to look your negative Ego in the eye, and take back control of your life, because if you don't then you may never free yourself from the negative ego and therefore, you will never truly be happy or successful. When deciding to break your first habit, don't make the mistake of using the mentality of "all or nothing." Your negative habits have been in control for years, and so you will need to be smart, diligent, ruthless, and patient to take back control.

First, decide today that you will make a change. Next, plan your work, and then work your plan *sensibly, responsibly and ruthlessly*.

FOR MORE IN-DEPTH STUDY OF THIS CHAPTER, PLEASE VISIT www.77GlobalVillage.com

STUCK IN THE TRENCHES
(Chapter 6 - Week 6)

"One of the most common reasons so few people are consistently able to achieve meaningful results is that they are unwilling to experience the discomfort associated with relentlessly pursuing a correct perception of reality."

- Stuart Brodie

If you first did not succeed in breaking your habit then try, try again, with greater determination, discipline and push yourself through "struggle" to the other side. It can be done.

All these weeks have been about building the student's confidence that they are going to be okay. In real life, it's so essential to have that inner confidence, and improvisation classes are a great way to get you up and performing. These types of classes help you discover your willingness to have fun, try risk-taking and just make it up as you go.

Improvisation is also an excellent, multilayered tool, which can be used for team collaboration or personal development. Improvisation also has many business applications like listening to your client's needs, reacting positively, and then helping your customers get what they want. This type of thinking is essential to your business success. Try an improvisation class for yourself and have fun in the moment.

I also worked on the students' "stage presence." Now stage presence begins with your personality. You need to be feeling strong within and then think of something funny which creates a natural smile. When you walk across that stage or enter a room, you enter standing tall and walk with an "air of confidence" that says; *"This is who I am!"*

What's So Special About You?

For an exercise, I had the students knock on a door, enter the room and walk twenty feet across the floor to their mark, trying to look relaxed and confident, all the while being scrutinized by their peers seated as casting people.

Then the other students would offer their personal thoughts and impressions on how that person entered the room. Did they enter too "cocky" or did they look intimidated? Did they enter with style or look awkward? Did they enter with an air of natural confidence? Or did they walk across the floor like a mouse? This was the time for the students to see how they are perceived by others when they enter a room. They also had to be willing to listen to constructive criticism without getting upset or defensive.

This exercise takes "guts" because most people don't like being the object of attention. They don't like a critique, especially when they perceive it to be negative. People's inner defenses go up; they feel the pressure rise, and they shut down to any positive learning, which is the trap most of the students fell into when they tried this exercise. They entered the room more concerned about what others were thinking of them instead of feeling confident, successful, charged up and ready to have some fun in the moment.

My question to you is: What's the lesson for you in all this?

Meanwhile on the next page is your next round of success qualities. No excuses now, just stay focused, take your time and answer honestly.

Chapter 6 ~ Stuck In The Trenches

HOW DO YOU RATE WITH THE BEST – ROUND 6

Below are the next 8 empowering qualities that the world's most successful people use to create fabulous happiness and success. How do you rate? **Remember, the box on the left (#1) is empowering, and (#5) is self-defeating, and (#3) is halfway.**

1	2	3	4	5

Successful people tend to have or be:

39/Mastered the Message: They have learned how to master their corporate message and the message about themselves, so the world sees what they want the world to see of them. Do people see YOU as lazy, unreliable, loud-mouthed, a hot-head, a slave driver, or unapproachable? Or do they see you as cool-headed, sincere, driven, a real leader, confident and trustworthy? [How well do you control your personal message?]

40/Teach: They are great teachers. They offer life experience, wisdom and the disciplined approach to building both your inner and outer success. Listen to Jack Welch, legendary chairperson / CEO of General Electric and Fortune's "Manager of the Century" title in 2000 - "As a leader, you have to have a teachable point of view." [On what scale are you the Teacher?]

41/ Persistent: They have an ability to endure in the face of adversity. They will keep going forward no matter how hard the hit. They will continue through the struggle, continue to get-up, continue their constant effort - continue, continue, continue! [How persistent are you through adversity?]

42/ Goal Focused: They aim high. They have clarity on the goals they strive for. They are not impressed with how long you have dedicated your life towards something. They want to know if you achieved results. [How clear is your focus on your objectives?]

What's So Special About You?

43/ Emotionally Competent: They are able to feel and express their emotions in a healthy and constructive way. No need to feel like you are walking on eggshells around this person. [How well do you express yourself?]

44/ Enterprising: They combine imagination; initiative and resourcefulness to problem solve issues and make great things happen in a positive direction. [How enterprising are you?]

45/Resourceful: They are good at problem-solving and being able to dig up whatever they need, from God knows where. They have learnt to be resourceful. [How resourceful are you?]

46/ Seek Opportunities: They know that opportunity is prosperity and they are always open to opportunity knocking at their door. They sense unique ideas and concepts that they could use in a way that nobody else has thought of. In fact, their mind has been conditioned to see possible business opportunities everywhere.

What's your score for round 6?

From the total of 8 questions, tally up and give yourself a 1, 2, 3, 4, or 5 for each tick you placed in the appropriate box as below.

1	2	3	4	5

Can you see where you are on par with the world's most successful people? Where do you need improvement?

Chapter 6 ~ Stuck In The Trenches

THE BOTTOM LINE:

Stop limiting yourself with excuses, because excuses will always be there for you, but opportunity won't.

Think of how many times you limit yourself with one excuse or another, and rob yourself of the opportunities that can change your life. *In stark contrast, the world's most successful people don't limit themselves; instead, they pursue an opportunity like lions! They strive to place a flag on the mountain of life and business. They don't believe in excuses, they believe in themselves, and they believe in positive results.*

It may take considerable effort for the mind and body to get familiar with new changes, and when the changes are coming daily, you MUST keep *consistently* pushing yourself forward through the struggle and stop the excuses. It's during this "struggle" that the body and mind may offer up heavy resistance, better known as excuses, but you MUST press on, grind on if you must, but make progress.

This is where most people give up, in that area of "resistance" or the "struggle." This is where most people feel like they just can't do it. They feel drained, worn down and they surrender with lots of excuses in their "defense."

Remember the movie "The Truman Show" with Jim Carrey? If Truman went with the flow or took the path of least resistance, he would never have got into that boat and sailed away from his hometown, from his place of security, comfort and knowing. Even when the massive life-threatening storm hit him and his little boat, most of us would have said, this is not meant to be, it's the universes' way of saying "Turn back now!" But Truman followed his heart and pushed through all his fears and made the breakthrough that changed his life forever.

If you continue through your own personal storm making no excuses, you will make a life-changing breakthrough, and that breakthrough will be proof positive that *"YES, I CAN DO THIS!"*

Once you believe in you, the excuses will stop, and you will learn to listen through the static and hear your intuition. Then miracles will happen, sometimes slowly, and sometimes in the blink of an eye.

What's So Special About You?

The point is this: when you make positive changes to your life, success happens, and that success will build upon success and your life changes. You will feel happier!

This message is the key!

It's the key that the world's most successful people have proved over and over again throughout history!

This is their message for you to follow.

Where most people give up on themselves when faced with the "struggle," *successful people keep going, adjusting to any setbacks they face, and their belief in themselves never waivers.* IT NEVER FALTERS!

In the words of Steve Jobs: *"The ones that were successful loved what they did so they could persevere when it got really tough. The ones that didn't love it quit."*

**FOR MORE IN-DEPTH STUDY OF THIS CHAPTER,
PLEASE VISIT www.77GlobalVillage.com**

Chapter 7 ~ Facing Inner Risk

FACING INNER RISK
(Chapter 7 – Week 7)

"It seems that people have vast potential. Most people can do extraordinary things if they have the confidence or take the risks. Yet most people don't. They sit in front of the telly and treat life as if it goes on forever."

- Philip Adams

An ordeal, test or crucible can take many forms; with some being life-threatening, or violent, or can be more mundane moments of self-doubt or failure. But whatever the nature of the crucible, it can be an inspiring story of how you were challenged, met that challenge head on and became a better person as a result. Build a legacy or you can just wither away.

The "Gladiatorial Games" are where each student's level of stress finally meets their training and confidence. In other words, it's time to put the training to the test for some real stakes. Real auditions are the arena, the crucible, where hundreds of actors meet daily to *act-it-out* against each other, in the hopes of getting a role, be it a film or television role, or a voice-over for a cartoon or a commercial. The competition is fierce. No mercy is asked for, and none is given.

This arena is also like the business arena where the world's most successful people do battle, trading in stocks, bonds, shares, acquiring companies, wheeling, dealing and competing for the opportunities that the world of business has to offer. We all know it can be cut-throat. Only one will win a role, will win the promotion or that new job, while the others must face that awful feeling of rejection, along with that spirit-sucking reality called a *mediocre life.*

What's So Special About You?

The students know that this week will be hard, but they have no idea just how demanding and challenging it's really going to be.

For the Gladiatorial Games, the students must participate in two auditions per day or receive a "fail" on their report card. They each get the same audition, and, as in an actual audition situation, each student must wait outside as one student at a time is brought into the room to perform their work. When everyone is finished, students sit together to review each other's audition. After viewing an audition, the student in question now stands up in front of the class and receives *"constructive criticism"* from each of the other students and from me. This is where your ego must just lay down and die because being egotistical or defensive here will go hard against you. It's called eating "humble pie." Students would be wise to listen and learn.

Once everyone has their say, they all cast a very important vote on a scale of 1 to 10, with "10" being an amazing performance. Once all students have gone through this process of review, critique and the votes recorded, the actors break to prepare for the next audition.

During this break time, I calculate votes to see who won first, second and third places. The actor who wins first place gets an "A" on their report card, a "B" for second place, and a "C" for third. All other scores lower than the top three aren't worth mentioning. Yes, it's tough, just like real life, and the message is the same: *"If you really want it, then get off your ass and apply yourself 150%; otherwise get out of the way".*

> **"Experience is the hardest kind of teacher.
> It gives you the test first and the lesson afterward."**
> - Oscar Wilde

The Gladiatorial Games become more stressful as they go on because no one wants to be out of the top three positions. Everyone wants to be first, and no one wants to be last, and as the games continue, friends become fierce competitors in the audition arena.

Each one is performing for their piece of the dream which says, *"If you can't win here, what hope is there of winning an audition in the real world, where your dream is on the line?"*

Chapter 7 ~ Facing Inner Risk

In truth, the games are not about winning or losing; the games are about taking risks, accepting rejection and getting back up. *The games are about being fully prepared and then learning to fail so you can learn to win.*

Some lessons are best learned not through words but through actual experience. The world's most successful people are willing to face "uncomfortable" situations all the time, and they make the changes needed to be on the top of their game. **Remember, the box on the left (#1) is empowering, and (#5) is self-defeating, and (#3) is halfway.**

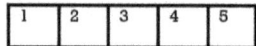

Let's see how well you do with the next set of 8 qualities.

How do you rate with the best – ROUND 7

Successful people tend to be or have:

47/ Apply Yourself: They know how to apply themselves fully to get something done. They understand that "Knowing is not enough; **we must apply**. Willing is not enough; **we must do**." Johann Wolfgang von Goethe. [On what scale do you apply yourself]

48/ Responsible: They are conscientious, trustworthy and offer themselves up for accountability. [How responsible are you?]

49/ Collaborative: They are able to work very well with others in creating a team dynamic that is often harmonious and inspiring. [How good are you at creating a team dynamic that is harmonious and inspiring?]

50/ Skilled Negotiators: They are experts at applying the win-win formula. [How well do you apply the win-win formula?]

What's So Special About You?

51/Salesmanship: The world's most successful people have a keen sense of selling without "selling." They know that selling is about knowing your stuff, knowing your uniqueness, building a relationship, having a real conversation where your words and energy paint a picture that excites anticipation. [How good are you at selling?]

52/Competitive: They have developed a healthy mindset for competition. They are willing to play hard, play fast, outwit, outlast and win gold and they expect the same from you. Remember, competition breaks limitations. [How competitive are you?]

53/Adaptive: They can adjust to the many changes faced in order to achieve their goals. In fact, they have built their empires on being adaptive. [How adaptive are you?]

54/Risk-Takers: They are not afraid to fail. They know that even if you are "wise to success," you will always learn more from "failing" then you ever will from winning. The only time you truly "fail" is when you have learned nothing from the experience. They know you can always learn something from any experience if you are truly honest and open. They are responsible risk takers. [How much of a risk taker are you?]

What's your score for round 7?

From the total of 8 questions, tally up and give yourself a 1, 2, 3, 4, or 5 for each tick you placed in the appropriate box as below.

1	2	3	4	5

Can you see where you are on par with the world's most successful people? Where do you need improvement?

Chapter 7 ~ Facing Inner Risk

MEANWHILE: BACK IN CLASS

The Gladiatorial auditions were packed with deadlines, stress, and challenges. It had its moments of being god-awful, funny, embarrassing, fearful, enlightening, great and inspiring. It almost sounds like most of our typical work weeks, doesn't it?

However, having said all that, the students went through the meat-grinder to learn by the experience because *success starts within you, and it can be whatever you want "success" to be.* **You have the power.**

Unfortunately, most people cower behind FEAR and never really push through it to the other side to experience the real feeling of achievement, happiness, and success. Instead, they choose to live a mediocre life and convince themselves they are happy.

There will always be elements of risk in anything you undertake, and the world's most successful people have tasted defeat many times. They have crashed and burned on so many occasions, and they chose to learn from the experiences because they knew what the rewards would be. *They know that to "face risk" is to help them live their dreams. So, learn to "face risk" on your own terms, and you will succeed. But if you have to face risk that is NOT on your terms then adapt; fail if you must but come back stronger and wiser.*

I want you to read the quotes on the next page, and realize they are words forged from *bitter experiences that offer YOU inspiring insight and powerful wisdom!*

These words have been lived! They are words that say "You are not alone" when facing risk each day because the world's most successful people that came before you have been there. They know what you're feeling, thinking and doubting. They have failed, and they have tried again, and they have overcome and so will YOU.

That's their message.

What's So Special About You?

Hold these words of experience true to your heart's desire… never let them go.

> *"I've failed over and over again in my life and that is why I succeed."*
>
> ~ Michael Jordan

> *"Success is stumbling from failure to failure with no loss of enthusiasm."*
>
> ~ Sir Winston Churchill

> *"There is only one thing that makes a dream impossible to achieve: the fear of failure."*
>
> ~ Paulo Coelho, The Alchemist

> *"It is hard to fail, but it is worse never to have tried to succeed."*
>
> ~ Theodore Roosevelt

> *"Only those who dare to fail greatly can ever achieve greatly."*
>
> ~ Robert F. Kennedy

> *"I have not failed. I have just found 10,000 things that do not work."*
>
> ~ Thomas Edison (on inventing electric light bulb)

> *"If at first, you don't succeed, try, try again."*
>
> ~ W.C. Fields

FOR MORE IN-DEPTH STUDY OF THIS CHAPTER, PLEASE VISIT www.77GlobalVillage.com

Chapter 8 ~ All The World's A Stage

ALL THE WORLD'S A STAGE
(Chapter 8 – Week 8)

*"Personality always did, always does,
and always will sell."*

Christopher Healy – Coach, presenter, and author.

In the new economy where information content is "king" and your personality is gold, you need to face your fears of public speaking and look into the lens of the camera, so you can <u>communicate</u> to your followers, supporters, clients and customers.

Now that the Gladiatorial games had ended the students could take a deep sigh of relief before tackling their next assignment - the "monologues." The Webster's dictionary definition of a monologue is a "dramatic sketch performed by one actor" and can be any length from 1 – 5 minutes. Most monologues are about 2 minutes in length.

Learning a monologue can feel like you're climbing up a mountain and can feel overwhelming at times, but you have to keep moving upwards.

Even to the most experienced executive, speaking in public can be a daunting thing, to say the least.

When ready, you walk out on stage in front of everyone watching you. You can hear a pin drop. Then you speak. Yikes!!

For actors, having a good monologue prepared may be their opportunity for a manager or agent to discover them, and get them out into the world of show business. However, for regular people, having an opportunity to tell someone about yourself can sometimes leave you "speechless," and how embarrassing is that?

What's So Special About You?

You are well advised to work out in advance what you would tell people about "you," and be prepared for when that opportunity may arise.

I am not going to dig too deep into the art of communication except to say that, *spoken communication* is our most powerful form of persuasion and as such, it's vital for not just actors, but for regular people, executives, managers, especially entrepreneurs to learn the art of *PRESENTATION*.

People, including actors, need to learn how to communicate with passion, clarity, authenticity, and influence. I hope you can see how showing your genuine personality for presentations on stage or on camera can benefit you greatly as an actor, businessman, manager, employee or an entrepreneur.

To quote a successful man named Brendon Burchard, the founder of "Experts Academy" and #1 New York Times and #1 USA Today bestselling author of **"The Millionaire Messenger"** and **"The Charge"** - *"Speaking is the only way to get your message out there. Now more than ever, you are selected from others based on what you say, how you say it, how you appear, and how real and authentic you are."*

And I will quote from another insightful book **"Celebrity Branding YOU"** by Nick Nanton and J.W. Dicks. *'People buy People'*, meaning it's all about your personality.

So, the message is the same for all of us: Follow in the footsteps of the world's most successful people by learning to overcome your fears, hang-ups, and self-doubts, and learn to be a master communicator. You will make great progress towards happiness and success.

Therefore, the best advice I can offer anyone in business, including actors, is to take courses in the following subjects:

- Public speaking
- On stage presentations
- Interviewing and giving interviews
- Presenting at sales meetings and conferences
- Online webinars and courses
- Direct to camera video presentations

Chapter 8 ~ All The World's A Stage

- Speeches and business pitches
- Presenting "shopping channel" style
- Presenting for Infomercials
- Doing TV commercials, even mock-up commercials.
- Speaking at media interviews
- Speaking for "coaching style."
- Speaking for DVD's
- Presenting "news broadcasting style"
- Walking into the room introductions
- Working on your image – how do you want to be seen?
- Take courses on inner healing of self. If you don't heal the inside, then your fears and hang-ups (about the way you look or sound) are still making you tense on camera. When on camera you want to be relaxed, letting your personality shine. If you are not relaxed, then your personality will not fully shine through to impress others in a positive light.

Finally, about the training list above, try some of them just to break out of being the typical, old you. For example, in my twenty plus years of teaching acting, I had in my classes all types of men and women, from ex-Russian soldiers, doctors, nurses, accountants, electricians, psychologists, university students, bankers, entrepreneurs, writers, directors, a prison guard and of course actors. All had their own reasons for trying something new, and all wanted to improve their lives. Most were willing to learn and try, while others wanted me to be their babysitter or, better yet, provide them with an excuse to say they tried and failed.

Do yourself a big, BIG favor and go try something new from the list I provided above. Go empower yourself.

Now, let's see if any of the next round of 7 empowering qualities from the world's most successful people are able to inspire you into breaking out of your old mold. **Remember, the box on the left (#1) is empowering, and (#5) is self-defeating, and (#3) is halfway.**

1	2	3	4	5

What's So Special About You?

HOW DO YOU RATE WITH THE BEST – ROUND 8

Successful people tend to be or have:

55/Communicators: They understand that *"communication in all its forms"* are powerful keys to success and happiness. However, this quality of "communication skills" drills deeper down to being *"articulate"* - speaking so that you are clearly understood is absolutely critical to your success. Articulate people know how to get to the point. Being articulate promotes their capacity of intelligentsia, education, culture, confidence and the higher echelons of potential leadership. There is almost a *"statesmanship"* like polish to this quality, and it is impressive. They can express thoughts, ideas, or feelings **coherently from their mind to you**, so you can understand exactly what they are thinking, which brings clarity to whatever the situation is. [How effective a communicator (not just a talker) are you?]

56/Tenacious: Meaning, they are a strategic thinkers who possess a will that refuses to submit. They will hold fast while making adjustments to achieve success. [How tenacious are you when the going gets tough?]

57/Storytellers: The world's most successful people know that a great story can take your breath away, spark-up your imagination, influence your energy to where you can actually see, feel and create any reality you want. [How good are you at storytelling?]

58/Persuasive: They know that if you can't get somebody to "Yes" then the exercise is a non-starter. So they have learned to apply all their qualities, skills and charms to the art of persuading somebody to say "Yes." [How effective are you at getting people to say "Yes"?]

59/Friendly: They create a pleasant and welcoming atmosphere through their character, their homes, at work and in their lives. [How friendly are you to create a welcoming atmosphere?]

Chapter 8 ~ All The World's A Stage

60/Open-Minded: They are open-minded enough to change their viewpoints, opinions or decisions according to circumstances. They stay open-minded and not closed off in a rut. Nothing for them is set in stone. [How open-minded are you?]

61/Wellbeing: They know that a peaceful body and mind allows for creativity, innovation, decision making, and opens a channel for their wisdom and intuitive insight. They exercise daily and meditate their minds, allowing for the renewal of body, mind, and spirit. [How well do you look after your health?]

What's your score for round 8?

From the total of 7 questions, tally up and give yourself a 1, 2, 3, 4, or 5 for each tick you placed in the appropriate box as below.

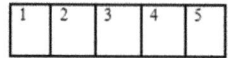

1	2	3	4	5

Can you see where you are on par with the world's most successful people? Where do you need improvement?

MEANWHILE: BACK IN CLASS

Apart from the monologues that the students had to do for this week, we also covered the promotional Demo Reel. A promotional DVD of 3 – 5 minutes in length of the actor's work is a critical tool for their self-promotional package. They use this DVD to get agents, managers, and acting work.

For my students, this was the most demanding part of the course because in order to get excellent quality DVD's we need real production. We need real cameras, lights, and plenty of re-shoots until they get it right. Also, the scenes that the students have chosen to perform must be right for them as a vehicle for showcasing their best qualities.

It was also around this time that the students were beginning to reveal their *inner conflicts* about moving on into the real world. The course was coming to an end, and soon they would be out there for real. Everything that these students have feared throughout this adventure fell away, only to make way for new fears, new unknown challenges to come.

The difference now, however, is that each of them *believes* that no matter what life throws at them they have the tools that will allow them to *push through,* and remain on their own path to happiness and success.

Isn't this what we all want to believe in our own hearts?

This is a huge change in these students' lives, and they can feel it. This change will stay with them for the rest of their lives, and hopefully, inspire others to live their dreams to the fullest.

FOR MORE IN-DEPTH STUDY OF THIS CHAPTER, PLEASE VISIT www.77GlobalVillage.com

EAT. DRINK. ENJOY!
(Chapter 9 – Week 9)

"It is health that is the real wealth."
Mahatma Gandhi

 **Your health and Intellect are the two blessings in life, and how you use them or abuse them will provide your life with abundant prosperity or lingering despair.**

Well, all good things must come to an end, and this was the last week for the students to be together. Their time went fast, and they became emotional during these last days.

Striving for your personal best can take its toll on anyone. That's why your health is an important part of your endurance and your sanity. I had suggested to the students on many occasions that they eat nutritious food and get plenty of rest because they were going to need it, not just for this course, but for the long haul of life.

The lesson from the world's most successful people is that you must stay healthy above all else. If you smoke, give up. If you're overweight, lose it. If you're feeling run down, then liven-up, get motivated, get jazzed, get juiced, get going!

Go to the gym, run, walk, dance, jump rope; do Martial Arts, Yoga, play soccer. Do whatever you need to do, or love to do, and go do it.

Each morning you wake up healthy, you are blessed, and you had better take advantage of that health because it won't last forever.

What's So Special About You?

Now, let's see if any of the next round of 8 empowering qualities from the world's most successful people are able to inspire you into breaking out of your old mold. **Remember, the box on the left (#1) is empowering, and (#5) is self-defeating, and (#3) is halfway.**

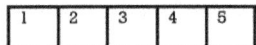

How do you rate with the best – ROUND 9

Successful people tend to be or have:

62/Visionary: They are willing to grasp new concepts, think BIG, dream BIG, invest and shape the future - their own future or even yours. They look ahead and ask "Imagine If?" They look at what people's future needs will be and provide them. Sometimes they will shape the future by creating the "stimulus," like a revolutionary product or a new market that then invokes the people's "Need" to get it. [On what scale are you a visionary?]

63/Intuitive: The world's most successful people listen, trust and take action on their own inner guidance or inherent instinct towards fantastic success. Oprah, Steve Jobs, and Conrad Hilton are just three to tell you that they built their empires on listening and acting on their intuition. [How much do you truly listen to your gut instincts?]

64/Curious: They are curious enough to ask questions, seek help or advice. They want to know how things work and use "solution-focused" questions to think clearly and overcome many challenges. [How comfortable are you with asking people for help?]

65/Strategic Thinkers: They can express the big vision, blend creativity and innovation, leverage ideas, think through consequences, and be proactive, work through decisions based on evidence and some calculated hunches to create fabulous success. [How much of a strategic thinker are you?]

Chapter 9 ~ Eat. Drink. Enjoy!

☐☐☐☐☐ **66/ Self-reflective:** They take time to think and reflect on themselves; their feelings, actions, failures, and successes. They know that only through honest and constructive **self-reflection** will you gain the insights, perspective, and understanding needed to begin the process of transformation towards success and happiness. [How deeply do you self-reflect?]

☐☐☐☐☐ **67/ Creative:** They're able to make imaginative use of limited recourses or use their imagination to create new ideas or things and use a creative approach to problems/situations. [On what scale do you consider yourself creative?]

☐☐☐☐☐ **68/ Self-Aware:** They understand the concept of "know thyself," including their skills, values, interests, strengths, weaknesses, behaviors and their strength of character. [How well do you know yourself?]

☐☐☐☐☐ **69/ Self-Worth:** They have cultivated a set of high values that they live by. They embrace these personal values to guide their lives moment to moment and are the cornerstones of their strength of character, their integrity and their personality. These high values define their self-worth. [On the scale, how is your self-worth?]

What's your score for round 9?

From the total of 8 questions, tally up and give yourself a 1, 2, 3, 4, or 5 for each tick you placed in the appropriate box as below.

1	2	3	4	5

Can you see where you are on par with the world's most successful people? Where do you need improvement?

What's So Special About You?

MEANWHILE: BACK IN CLASS

This course has been hard for the students. They have stepped into an environment that each day pushed them to their limits, and yet, demanded even more from them. They have had to focus like never before, and push through their crap to produce something of worth within themselves, something that says *"YES - I can do this. I can do anything"*. Now, in the last week, they've got to reach even deeper because the summit is only steps away.

They still have a ton of work to complete; shoot the final scenes for their promotional DVD reels featuring their best work, including their comedy and drama monologues. The students had to learn to do many "takes" of each scene until the right moment was captured on camera, and then we moved onto setting up for the next reaction shots. It was a lot of hard work, and it keeps the students on their toes and mentally engaged.

The hardest part was the monologues. They had to use their newly found skills to break down the monologues and find insights into their characters. Then "on camera" they had to be real and live truthfully in the moment.

The students had truly found their working rhythm and were eager to drive it all the way home to a finish.

It's clear that the students have come full circle, only to come face to face with their past selves. Many times this week, they talked of when they first entered the class, with their doubts, fears, and hopes.

The road they journeyed these past 9 weeks has led them back to the beginning where it all started. Almost like looking at themselves in the mirror for a second time, except this time they could see the changes in their eyes, and, more importantly, they could feel the changes within.

Chapter 9 ~ Eat. Drink. Enjoy!

The students had completed all their tasks with flying colors. Each of them has stepped up to the opportunity *to rebuild, renovate and improve their lives for the better.*

Some inspiring lines from the students that stay with me included what Chrissy said: *"I am free. I am powerful. I am alive!"* And also what Tab said.... *"Then I can leave with the knowledge that I can build bridges, and I can build them to take me anywhere I want to go."*

The above is truly powerful words to live by. I hope that you will embrace the following words as part of your legacy.

"*I am Alive. I am Healthy. I am Free.*"

Think about that for a moment. You are alive. Now ask yourself, what's the quality of your life? Are you healthy or not-so-healthy?

How important is health to you?

What's So Special About You?

EAT. DRINK. ENJOY!

Let's explore the three life nurturing elements of *eat, drink, enjoy*.

1 Eat plenty of nutritious organic foods

2 Drink lots of water

3 Enjoy your restful sleep

FYI, the better you sleep, the better you can deal with the next day. See below for the negative effects of lack of sleep, because it's all relative to your quality of life and the decisions you make.

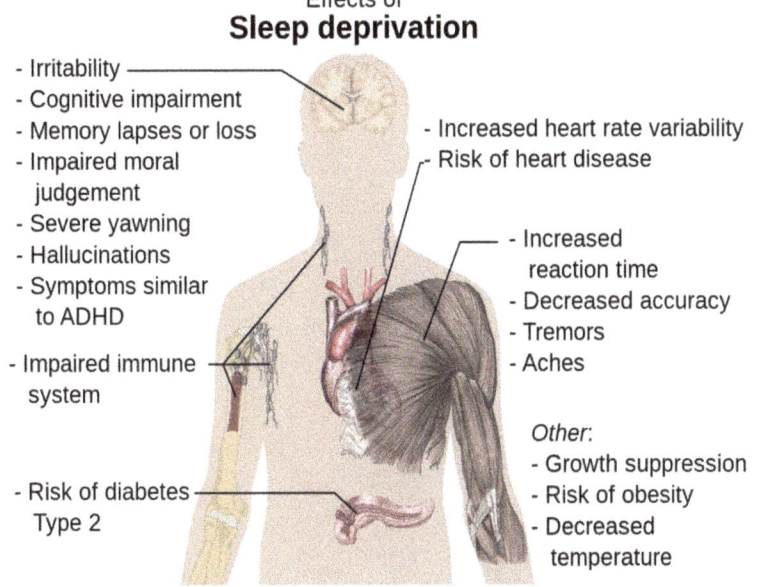

Sleep specialists suggest that you need to sleep between 7-9 hours a day to achieve your personal optimal morning *"start-up"* so you can last the whole day. Don't be using coffee or other stimulants to get you *"up and going"* because they will only bring you down until you take another hit of *"pick-me-up."*

113

Instead, *practice and discipline yourself* to starting your day with an inspiring visualization followed by whatever gets you out of bed ready to go, and please keep your personal *"wellness"* factor in mind.

WHY DRINK WATER?

Well, obviously, water has a life-saving role to play in keeping our bodies in high spirits. In fact, your body is 70% water, and without adequate water consumption, your body begins to break down. For example, below are the major reasons why you need to stay well hydrated.

- reduces the risk of cancer
- easier digestion
- helps to lose weight
- nourishes healthy skin
- helps fights infection
- gets rid of body toxins
- promotes a healthy heart
- lubricates your joints
- prevents pains and arthritis
- prevents constipation
- improves your overall productivity
- is a natural remedy for headaches
- allows for better exercise
- relieves fatigue
- protects your body organs and tissue
- helps kidneys and liver by flushing out waste products
- boosts energy
- regulates body temperature
- lessens the likelihood of illness

Signs and symptoms of mild dehydration include:

- thirst
- dry lips and mouth
- flushed skin
- tiredness
- irritability
- headache
- dizziness
- fainting
- low blood pressure
- increased in heart rate
- dark, strong-smelling urine

Signs of severe dehydration include:

- blue lips
- blotchy skin
- confusion
- lack of energy
- cold hands and feet
- rapid breathing
- high fever
- unconsciousness.

Health authorities commonly recommend eight, 8-ounce glasses, which equals about 2 liters, or half a gallon. This is called the 8×8 rule and is very easy to remember.

There are many professionals who believe that you should simply sip water throughout your day. It's even being suggested that if you become dehydrated not only does your energy levels drop, but more troubling, that your brain functions will begin to be affected.

There are plenty of studies that support this. In fact, some studies have shown that mild dehydration caused by exercise or excessive heat can negatively affect other aspects of our brain functions. So, make sure you stay hydrated for all the right reasons.

Chapter 9 ~ Eat. Drink. Enjoy!

NUTRITIOUS FOODS

Nutritious foods are essential to your happiness and success. Take a look at these nutritious food combinations for a healthier you.

 Tomatoes can reduce the risk of cancer and cardiovascular disease when eaten with avocado.

 This combination of Broccoli plus Tomato helps prevent prostate cancer according to recent Cancer studies.

 We all know the goodness of Vitamin C but did you know that when taken with plant-based foods the vitamin C makes the iron nutrient more absorbable?

Below are other excellent reasons as to why you should eat as much fruit as you can in developing your body, mind, and spirit of happiness and success.

What's So Special About You?

Did you know that Cancer Research confirms that currently, 7.6 million people die from cancer worldwide every year, out of which, 4 million people die prematurely (aged 30 to 69 years). That's a staggering amount of people and families whose lives are ruined by this deadly scourge.

Tumors and refined sugar are a breeding ground for Cancer. *Choose "natural sugars' over refined* sugar. Stay away from artificial sweeteners especially Aspartame, which is considered "sweet poison" for a good reason. Stay away from "Fructose." Refined sugars provide "empty" or "naked" calories and lack the natural minerals which are present in natural sugars. **Aspartame is poison pure and simple.**

I strongly suggest you do your own research on this. Check out the cancer research on **The Secrets of Sugar - The Fifth Estate - CBC.ca** https://youtu.be/9mzf4KSG6oQ

So please get to work on any kind of daily physical exercise, along with eating fresh, nutritious food, drinking plenty of water and sleeping well.

Chapter 9 ~ Eat. Drink. Enjoy!

When you take action on what you have discovered in this chapter, you'll find not only that your health will improve, but that will your overall wellbeing will increase to an optimal state.

Your confidence will soar to new heights, and you will feel like a whole new you! This is the core of your happiness and success, because without a healthy body, mind, and spirit then what have you got? Healthy living is what the world's most successful people LIVE BY, and they STRIVE for it.

This way of life MUST be your way of life.

For the students, school is out with the understanding that's as one of them put it, *"The next step we take is more important than the footprints we leave behind."*

The above statement is very true for them, and it is also very true for you. When you finally close this book, you will either fall back into the old ways which brought you here in the first place, or you will continue to work consistently and successfully forward!

What's So Special About You?

Remember, one degree of change changes your life!

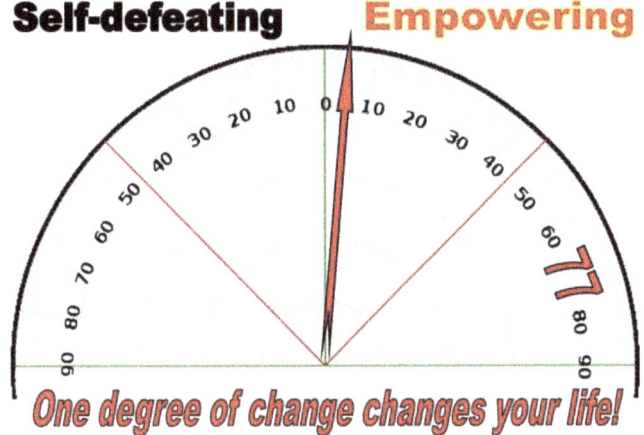

SCHOOL IS OUT!

FOR MORE IN-DEPTH STUDY OF THIS CHAPTER PLEASE AND FINAL HOME STUDY ASSIGNMENTS PLEASE VISIT www.77GlobalVillage.com

Chapter 10 ~ What's So Special About You?

EPILOGUE:
Chapter 10 ~What's So Special About You?

"I knew there was a way out. I knew there was another kind of life because I had read about it. I knew there were other places, and there was another way of being."

Oprah Winfrey

Always remember: you are not your past, so learn from your life's experiences to make better decisions that strengthens your inner power and your passion to improve your life, and in turn, you change the world for the better. **Make this your legacy that you will honor, live and share, always.**

I wanted to say that I know I have mentioned a lot of the world's most successful people throughout this book, and at times it may have felt like you were never going to be in their seemingly "perfect" league.

The truth is, we are All a work in progress. All of us are constantly evolving. I am offering you a proven path towards a beacon of light, and how to direct your evolution towards success and happiness based on that light composed of the 77 qualities and behaviors of the world's most successful people.

They know how to get there, so follow the light and experience the miracles happening in your life as it has happened in theirs.

The bottom line is this: the more comfortable you are with yourself, the more confident you will become, and that involves having a lot of *fun* doing what you love to do. *That's your happiness and success all rolled-up into one.*

What's So Special About You?

I will end the students work here with this final quote from Tab:

Take off your own mask.

"I think the biggest lesson I learned from this course was to simplify, and trust. There is so much that this translates to. It means when acting, seeing your character as simply another person, getting to know that person, and trusting that once you understand him or her enough if you play it real, you will have a portrayal worth watching.

It means looking at tests as assessments, whose purpose is to show you in what areas you are weak or strong, not massive hurdles whose aim is to trip you up and make you look bad, and auditions as a chance to go have fun with a mini-audience, with the possibility of winning a role.

It means looking at the people around you as people with the same amount of vulnerability beneath their outward appearances, and trusting that you will not be torn apart by the world if you take off your own mask. **I see it all now as an opportunity for me or for you to be your best, show who you are and what you can be."**

WOW! What a great last line, and isn't it true?

So, let me ask you, what does "opportunity" mean to you?

Chapter 10 ~ What's So Special About You?

Below is what some of the world's most successful people say about "opportunity." See if you agree with them.

"A pessimist sees the difficulty in every opportunity; an optimist sees the opportunity in every difficulty."

Winston Churchill

"Opportunity is missed by most people because it is dressed in overalls and looks like work."

Thomas A. Edison

"Ability is nothing without opportunity."

Napoleon Bonaparte

"One secret of success in life is for a man to be ready for his opportunity when it comes."

Benjamin Disraeli

"Failure is the opportunity to begin again more intelligently."

Henry Ford

Please take the above words to heart because they will change your life – guaranteed.

What's So Special About You?

How do you rate with the best — FINAL ROUND 10

Now, let's see if any of the next round of 7 empowering qualities from the world's most successful people are able to inspire you into breaking out of your old mold. **Remember, the box on the left (#1) is empowering, and (#5) is self-defeating, and (#3) is halfway.**

1	2	3	4	5

Below are the final 8 qualities. Let's see how well you do.

Successful people tend to:

70/Claim Ownership: They take ownership for what they do, and they expect you to do the same. If you were to ask an average person why they have been successful, they would usually use the words "I" and "Me." However, when you ask them why they failed at something, they make excuses and blame everything on others rather than take ownership of it. The bottom line here is that the world's most successful people take ownership of their lives. [On what scale do you take ownership of your life?]

71/Higher Purpose: They know in their heart why they do what they do. Their life's purpose is what drives their internal engine, and the big difference about the world's most successful people is that *their life's purpose empowers, motivates and inspires them to drive forward through all obstacles and challenges in greater service of others* and not in greater service of themselves. They understand that what they do benefits them greatly; however, they also know that what they do is a part of something much bigger than themselves. [On what scale is your life's purpose (assuming you know it) in greater service of others?]

72/Achieve Excellence: The world's most successful people strive for excellence in all they do. It's not *"my way or the highway thinking"* nor is it *"perfection,"* however, it is their uncompromising spirit that compels them to "excel" in life and inspires others to do the same. [How much do you achieve excellence?]

123

Chapter 10 ~ What's So Special About You?

☐☐☐☐☐ **73/ Contribute:** They contribute to society, volunteering their time, expertise or money to help others in their local community, or through charities into the world community. They mentor those that step up. [How much do you contribute to society or your local community?]

☐☐☐☐☐ **74/ Over-Deliver:** They over-deliver in their efforts. They know that anyone who can over-deliver is worth gold because most people deliver on the line, if at all. Successful people go that extra mile, even if it's the hardest mile. If you are prepared to over-deliver, you will be on the path to becoming remarkable and successful yourself. They go that extra mile! If you are prepared to go that extra mile and over-deliver, you will be stepping into the shoes of the world's most successful people and on the path to becoming remarkable and successful yourself. [How far along that extra mile, are you prepared to venture?]

☐☐☐☐☐ **75/The Pioneering Spirit:** The world's most successful people love adventure. They break limitations and push themselves forward, past their comfort zones and into the unknown. From reaching the bottom of the sea to the highest peaks, or across the oceans to new lands or new worlds. From creating new technologies to breaking new boundaries in science. It's the broad shoulders of these giants that have and will continue to advance ALL human civilization. Now that's a big deal. [How much of the pioneering spirit do you have?]

☐☐☐☐☐ **76/Passionate:** They are passionate about what they do. It feeds their soul, changes lives, and they earn a fabulous lifestyle from it. Most people work for a living and save what they love to do for some other time. [How passionate are you about your work or your career?]

☐☐☐☐☐ **77/Forgive:** The world's most successful people have learned to forgive and move on with free-flowing energy to create spectacular success and happiness. Let go of the past. Let go of the pain, the regret, whatever it is that weighs heavy on your heart, but most of all forgive yourself first.

What's So Special About You?

What's your score for round 10?

From the total of 8 questions, tally up and give yourself a 1, 2, 3, 4, or 5 for each tick you placed in the appropriate box as below.

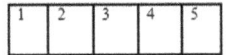

Can you see where you are on par with the world's most successful people? Where do you need improvement?

The above 77 qualities represent successful people like, Sir Richard Branson, Oprah Winfrey, Tony Robbins, Giorgio Armani, Bill Gates, Steve Jobs, Steven Spielberg, Quincy Jones, Martin Luther King, Mahatma Gandhi, Viola Davis, Yani Tseng, Freeman Hrabowski, Marc Andreessen, Sara Blakely, Eike Batista, Winston Churchill, Ronald Reagan, Margaret Thatcher, Henry Ford, David Rockefeller, Morgan, Thomas Edison, Arianna Huffington, and Nelson Mandela just to name a tiny, tiny few. Google their names, get their biographies and learn their personal stories for inspiration.

Okay, let's be honest with ourselves, the list of party-goers above are the types of people you should meet and make your best friends.

I know that people everywhere have many of the same winning characteristics mentioned throughout this book. However, where successful people separate themselves from others is that they understand that their lives are their own personal responsibility. *Embracing all 77 qualities is a complete lifestyle-defining-responsibility that will completely uplift your life - guaranteed!*

It's this "responsibility," or "taking ownership" of their lives, which is at the heart of all their personal development, happiness and success.

The reality for everyone else is that we can either accept the following conditions:
- hope for the best
- live on autopilot
- be a slave to our negative habits
- behave unfairly to ourselves and others
- don't believe in ourselves, nor in what we can achieve

Chapter 10 ~ What's So Special About You?

- settle for second rate/ second best
- never live up to our full potential
- live a "happily numb" life in mediocrity

OR, we can be inspired to stand up for ourselves, and accept the responsibility for changing our lives in order to be truly happy and successful. Whatever you decide, each of us must accept that we are the only person responsible for our decisions and actions.

The truth is that taking personal responsibility for your life is the catalyst for your happiness and success.

I trust that you have already begun the process of change by working through this book. Please add up your **FINAL SCORES**.

It's my conclusion that after all these years of study into these very successful people, that the world's most successful people do way more than just be "results driven." When you combine all the above 77 qualities and live them as a lifestyle. These people exhibit what I call the Knack.

They have a talented and remarkable knack for creating abundance for themselves as well as for others. It doesn't matter where you drop them, they tend to land on their feet and slowly rise to the top. I am reminded of the original "Planet of the Apes" movie with Charlton Heston, when, along with his two comrades, they see "The new world" of passive people eating fruit and laying around frivolously. He says *"If this is the best they have, then we will be running this planet in six months."* Some people call them born lucky, but for the world's most successful people, building an empire of happiness, success and abundance has very little to do with luck, and everything to do with diligence and tenacity in their efforts to embrace an incredibly, inspiring and uplifting lifestyle, guided by all 77 empowering qualities. ALL of them combined into a vortex of success, failure, and success again. It's a heck of a mountain to climb – but they have proved to us over and over again that it can be done. So go try it!

WHERE DO YOU FIT ON THE SCALE?

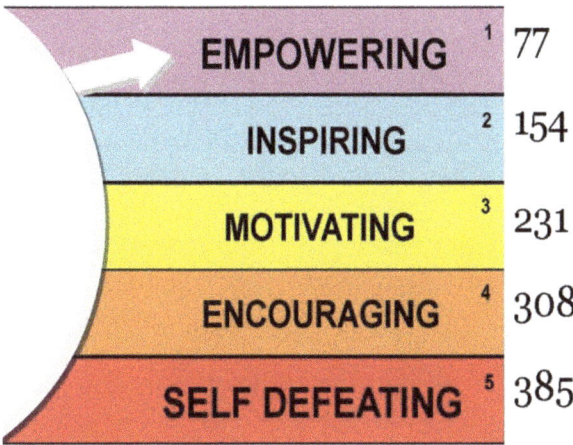

By the way, 77 is the "perfect" score, but then again, who's perfect? Definitely NOT the world's most successful people. However, as revealed in this book, they do "step up to the plate" and consistently hit incredible home runs based on all 77 success qualities!

You have completed the success by design challenge, and you now know where to improve and change your life in *small degrees*. Remember, your final scores to date are just the beginning of your journey of happiness and success.

Chapter 10 ~ What's So Special About You?

IN CONCLUSION: WHAT'S SO SPECIAL ABOUT YOU?

Learning about yourself is always a lifelong work in progress, and choosing to be the best you can be will always by your responsibility, your commitment and your bond with yourself. Own it, be it and do it. Choose to be a person of progress. I have learned that success and happiness are a daily decision. Each morning when I wake up, I shall see the morning sun and say to myself, *"I am alive. I am healthy. I am free. Now, what am I going to do with these three blessings today?"*

==**EMBRACE AS MANY OF THESE 77 SUCCESS QUALITIES AS YOU CAN. MAKE THEM WORK FOR YOU AT EMPOWERING LEVELS AND YOUR LIFE WILL CHANGE – GUARANTEED!**==

This is why successful people have mastered or are mastering all of the 77 winning success qualities. They use these strategies *consistently* to create success for themselves and here is the kicker, they are *always improving*. They understand that these success qualities are the "moving parts" or architecture behind who they are, and how they do what they do so consistently well. So, stop waiting for things to change. Stop waiting for the approval of others. *Move forward into your life's promise of success and happiness by taking actions that empower you and feed your soul one empowering degree at a time.*

The most successful people are those who believe that 100 percent of their success is up to them, and zero percent to outside conditions.

This type of "successful thinking" means that YOU do have the power to be successful and happy, for you have always had that power!

Believe it, for it is true, and within YOU!

You are now aware of the 77 winning qualities of the world's most successful people and how impactful and changing *even one of those qualities' can be to your life.*

You now have the 77 keys to open the doors.

Use them! And use them *consistently*.

What's So Special About You?

In conclusion: By working through and completing this book, you have now *left your mark on the sand* of what was once your old self; and have moved on to explore how fabulous your future can be... *the future of your choosing.*

That's what's so truly special about You!

You DO have the POWER to make a difference in your life, in your community, and in your world.

You have ALWAYS had this power!

That's a big, powerful and empowering statement to make on your behalf, and I don't even know you. However, in a way, I do know you. I know you want to be happy and successful, and I know you want to feel loved and share your love with your family and friends and add your own *personal touch* to this world.

So the truth that *you have always had this power* to make a real difference *is* the life-changing message from the world's most successful people, and from the students in this book. It's a powerful message for you to realize and to follow because now, you do have the 77 success qualities and you are now ready to take the lead from here on and add *your own personal touch.*

Chapter 10 ~ What's So Special About You?

At the end of the day, it doesn't matter if the students became "actors," because, in truth, all of us have many paths in life to follow. What is important is that they embrace the success qualities of the world's most successful people in their lives. They learn to give the best of themselves each day, and they learn to believe in themselves; that each of them can make a real difference in their own lives, and in the lives of the people they touched along the way.

They have inspired me to write this book, and it has changed my life, and, hopefully, it will change yours.

And in touching our lives with their beauty, each of those students is a very successful person indeed.

So get up and go explore your awesome future with confidence and brevity, and don't look back.

Cheers!

All the best from Christopher Healy.

The End.

What's So Special About You?

CLASSIC LOSERS ON THE JOURNEY TO SUCCESS!

To inspire you on your own personal journey, I would like you to read some of these all time "loser' success classics.

Henry Ford: When he was younger he failed at business and went broke many times and then went on to found the iconic Ford Motor Company.

Elvis Presley: One of the greatest performers of all time. When first starting out he was fired after just one performance at the Grand Ole Opry, being told by the manager that *"You ain't goin' nowhere, son. You ought to go back to drivin' a truck."*

Walt Disney: He was fired by a newspaper editor because he "lacked imagination and had no good ideas." He later started a number of businesses but failed at each of them. However, he went on to create Disney Theme Park, and of course, the rest is history.

Vincent Van Gogh: Considered one of the greatest painters of all time. He only sold one of his paintings to a friend. No others were sold until after his death.

Abraham Lincoln: He failed most of his life at most things, even getting demoted from being a Captain down to a Private while in the army. He failed at business, and like Churchill was defeated many times running for public office before becoming President of the United States, winning the American Civil War and freeing the slaves.

Harland David Sanders: He was fired from many jobs and even failed at selling his special secret chicken sauce over 1000 times until one day a restaurant accepted it, and he ended up creating the world-famous Kentucky Fried Chicken or KFC.

Oprah Winfrey: She was fired from her first television job as an anchor in Baltimore, where she said she faced sexism and harassment and later went on to become one of the most powerful women in America.

Albert Einstein: Einstein didn't speak until he was 4 and didn't read until age 7. His teachers and parents thought he was mentally handicapped. He was expelled from school and was refused admittance to the Zurich Polytechnic School.

Winston Churchill: He failed the sixth grade and had many political failures including being defeated in every election for public office until he finally became the Prime Minister at the age of 62.

Soichiro Honda: He started out making scooters from his home and went on to create the multi-billion dollar HONDA Company.

Richard Branson: Best known for his adventurous spirit and outrageous business tactics, he dropped out of school at 16 to start his first successful business venture; Student Magazine. He bought his own 79-acre Caribbean island when he was just 24 and was knighted in 1999. He is also the billionaire founder of the Virgin brand and its 360 companies. His companies include the famous Virgin Atlantic Airways.

Jerry Seinfeld: When he first went on stage as a stand-up comedian he froze and was booed off the stage but went on to become one of the most successful comedians ever, complete with his own hit TV show.

Charles Darwin: Darwin said, *"I was considered by all my masters and my father to be a very ordinary boy, rather below the common standard of intellect."*

Mary Kay Ash: Founder of Mary Kay Inc and best known as the most outstanding businesswoman in the 20th century. Mary never went to school! She said, *'When you reach an obstacle, turn it into an opportunity. You have a choice. You can overcome and be a winner, or you can allow it to overcome you and be a loser. The choice is yours and yours alone. Refuse to throw in the towel. Go that extra mile that failures refuse to travel. It is far better to be exhausted from success than to be rested from failure."*

Harrison Ford: When first starting out in movies, he was told by a movie executive that he didn't have what it takes to be a star.

Theodor Seuss Geisel: He was rejected 27 times before his first book Dr. Seuss's – *"To Think That I Saw It on Mulberry Street"* and the legendary, *"The Cat in the Hat"* or *"Green Eggs and Ham."*

What's So Special About You?

Steven Spielberg: He was rejected from the University of Southern California School of Theater, Film, and Television three times. The rest is iconic history.

Stephen King: *Carrie* was his first book, and it was rejected by publishers 30 times. He was so pissed off that he dumped it into the garbage. His wife took the book out of the trash and encouraged him to try again. King went on to become one of the bestselling authors of all time.

J. K. Rowling: She was depressed, divorced, on welfare and raised her kid while trying to write her book Harry Potter on napkins in her favorite coffee shop.

The Beatles: Decca Records top executive Dick Rowe rejected the Beatles saying that *"Groups with guitars are on the way out."*

Marilyn Monroe: She was first told by a top modeling agent to be a secretary.

Michael Dell: He dropped out of college at 19 to start PC's Limited; later renamed Dell Computers Inc. As you may know, Dell has become the most profitable PC manufacturer in the world making Michael Dell a multi-billionaire.

Andrew Carnegie: Andrew was born in extreme poverty that never included even going to school. No school at all! Yet Andrew became the founder of Carnegie Steel Company and became one of the richest men who ever lived.

Simon Cowell: He is famous for creating, producing and starring *(as the judge everybody loves to hate)* in American Idol. He actually dropped out of school at age 16 and at 23 started his own record label "Fanfare." "Good is not enough; you've got to be great." – Simon Cowell

Thomas Edison: If you can believe this, teachers told Edison that he was *"too stupid to learn anything."* He later went on to invent the electric light, the movie camera and further developed many other devices that greatly influenced life around the world.

WHAT'S SO SPECIAL ABOUT... NUMBER 77

Pythagoras of Samos has been described as a mathematician and philosopher. He was known as the father of Greek and Western Civilization. He said that everything in the universe was mathematically precise and that each number has its own essence or vibration and meaning.

As a matter of interest, in numerology, the number 77 represents personal freedom, but also that you are in tune with your Intuition and connected to the Universal Intelligence or Divine Wisdom.

Imagine having the inner freedom to pursue whatever interests you, because the number 77 means you are on the path to fulfilling your own destiny. *That's the power of 77.*

The number 77 is an Angel Number which indicates that you have listened to Divine guidance and are now putting that wisdom to work in your every day-to-day life. Your desires and wishes are coming to fruition in your life as a direct result of your actions and positive attitude to life and the time has come to reap the rewards for your diligence and determined efforts.

In religious numerology.

The Gospel of Luke lists 77 generations from Adam to Jesus and in certain numerological systems based on the English alphabet; the number 77 is associated with Jesus Christ. CHRIST is C = 3, H = 8, R = 18, I = 9, S = 19, T = 20, which added together equal 77

What's So Special About You?

WHAT'S SO SPECIAL ABOUT... CHRISTOPHER HEALY

December 2010, was not only the last class for the students, but it was also my last course. I have been the Artistic Director and principal acting teacher with the Toronto Academy of Acting for fifteen years. Now, I have stepped out into the world, living my dreams of specialty coaching, offering High-Performance solutions to companies, helping individuals discover their creative/innovative spark and writing a few books.

My final book in this series, **"What's So Special About US?"** is the natural follow-up to the first book *"What's So Special About You?"* except that it has a mysterious story as to how the book finally came about, including a dream-state revelation that blew my mind and changed my life.

In fact, how I got the end of the second book came from the years of exhaustive "back and forth" research for this book you are reading now.

What my research led me to uncover has profoundly influenced me, and it all happened one night while I was sleeping.

I had been obsessing for months about the final, chapter 10 of this book, *"What's' So Special About You?"* trying to find the "Capstone" that make this book exceptional.

I felt that years of research needed to be more than just words, but that didn't make any sense because I was writing a book, and a book has words. This nagging feeling had been "haunting" my mind for almost two months. Mentally I felt trapped in a maze.

I re-read all my thousands of notes on success, and read all the students journals again, trying to get a grip on anything, but I was

135

having no luck. I had no clues, no idea, nothing…zip. I just knew something different *"was in the air."*

Then one night, while sleeping, it happened around 4 am. My subconscious and conscious minds were fluctuating from one dream-realm to another. I was somewhere in the space between sleeping and waking. I remember some moments, still obsessing about the first book. Then, in the midst of my dreamscape, I saw vibrant colors of red, blue, yellow, green, violet, thereafter superimposed with images. They were all floating around within the colors. Nothing made sense. I could feel my breath in motion.

I knew I was "aware" and yet still sleeping. Then it happened.

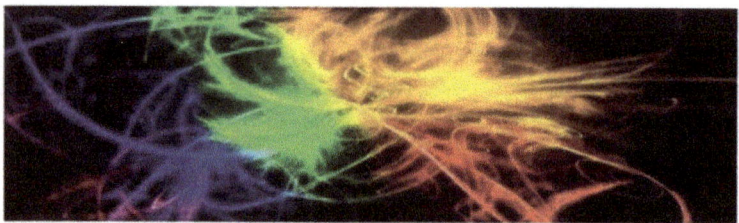

The vibrant images, colors, shapes and wording became clearer to me. I remember breathing deeply in and out through my nose. I felt so connected to a depth of relaxation. Then I saw the floating images; seeming to pull together in the form of a crest of symbols. It was at that moment that I realized the full revelation; this was something that was life-changing and previously unknown.

I opened my eyes, jumped out of bed, grabbed a pen, and began scribbling the crest of symbols, complete with colors and shading. It was like my mind was crystal clear, that I understood what I was drawing, even though it was almost dark, and I didn't have my glasses on. I just "knew the meanings" of the symbols, the secrets, what the true elements of success were, how they stimulated different parts of your brain to produce successful thinking.

I just knew what it all meant, and how to use it - *through which all success is manifested.*

I realized that what I intuitively invoked had never been seen before. When I felt sure I had is all down on paper as rudimentary as my drawings were, I put my glasses on and switched on the light. The feeling was electric, like reading an old treasure map. My eyes were scanning every line, every sketch, every symbol, and every word. I remember leaning back slightly, taking it all in.

These symbols were a deeper, more concentrated language, with significant meanings far beyond words in a book, and were profoundly more powerful, influential and life-changing. It was the most surreal experience I have ever had, and I knew I would try it again at a later time. If you know anything about the influence of symbols, especially in advertising, then you can appreciate that, instead of reciting positive affirmations to get me "all pumped up" in the morning. I can now look at the crest of symbols from which the core vibration elements of success radiates.

I name it, the "***Transcendence Crest©***" which synergizes and radiates the positive power of its influence to bring into play all the subconscious requirements needed to raise up my own vibration to that which embodies the vibration of successful thinking. I know it may seem a lot to take in it at first, but simply put, your mind is re-wired or powered-up to *think success, attract success* and *live success.*

It was the answer I was searching for.

Then I realized; ***it was also the answer you are searching for.***

I originally wanted all this work to be in one book, but that book was weighing in at over 600 pages! Therefore, I broke the research down as below for maximum effect in helping people.

1 / *Life Lessons From An Acting Class* is an eBook about Life Changing Insights as experienced and revealed in the personal accounts from the students themselves.

2 / *What's So Special About You?* (Learn the 77 success qualities from the world's most successful people) Book.

What's So Special About You?

Welcome to the
77 WINNING LIFESTYLE FORMULA COURSE

You receive the Book, 10 set Online Course and the e-Book.

3 / Online Course: Here I would take you step-by-step through the ten chapters of the book *"What's So Special About You"* and help you in applying consistently the winning qualities.

4 / *What's So Special About US?* This eBook is my "Crown Jewels" which reveal insights and teachings for anyone wanting to learn how best to empower themselves so they can do their part in helping change the world.

Sometimes we all get an opportunity to move our lives in a different direction. The students may not become actors but decide to become something else, and that's okay. They are free and confident to take whatever opportunities they desire. Whether you take your opportunity or not is your decision. I'm taking mine, and being able to use the 77 winning qualities in all we do, we are the keys to our own happiness and success. I'm going to have a fun ride, and I hope you do too!

Its time to live a more successful and happier life. You can always drop me a line and let me know what you think of my book, has it helped you in any way.

Thank you again for reading my book.

Bless and Dismiss.

Christopher Healy

What's So Special About You?

For over a decade now, I have been researching one question: How are the world's most successful people so finely tuned into the **frequency of success.** The answers I discovered cover five areas: your world, your health, your business, your mind, and interestingly enough the sensitivities of your intuitive spirit.

As part of my research for my books, I read every article and watched every interview on as many of the world's most successful and richest people from Bill Gates, Seth Godin, Oprah Winfrey and multitude of others over from all walks of life over this past decade.

So for my podcast / video show, instead of having the same people rehash their stories of success, I will open my podcast to the unknown successful people we have never heard of.

If you consider yourself a successful person, then I invite you to send me a one-page bio that describes your story, what do you do? What works for you? Tell us what led to the spark of your success? What's so special about you? Tell us; inspire us, share your wisdom so that we can learn from you.

I hope that my podcast / video show will provide you a platform to share your story of success, so that my listeners will be inspired into creating their own unique success stories. Please check out my new podcast / video show on www.77GlobalVillage.com

Together, let us tap into that frequency of success.

What's So Special About You?

www.ingramcontent.com/pod-product-compliance
Lightning Source LLC
Chambersburg PA
CBHW051548010526
44118CB00022B/2624